Karate's
Universal
Codeword

Karate's Universal Codeword

The Mysterious Origins, Meaning and Usage
of the Word "OSU" in the Martial arts

Toshinori Ohmori
Translated by Alexander Bennett

TUTTLE Publishing

Tokyo | Rutland, Vermont | Singapore

"Books to Span the East and West"

Tuttle Publishing was founded in 1832 in the small New England town of Rutland, Vermont [USA]. Our core values remain as strong today as they were then—to publish best-in-class books which bring people together one page at a time. In 1948, we established a publishing outpost in Japan—and Tuttle is now a leader in publishing English-language books about the arts, languages and cultures of Asia. The world has become a much smaller place today and Asia's economic and cultural influence has grown. Yet the need for meaningful dialogue and information about this diverse region has never been greater. Over the past seven decades, Tuttle has published thousands of books on subjects ranging from martial arts and paper crafts to language learning and literature—and our talented authors, illustrators, designers and photographers have won many prestigious awards. We welcome you to explore the wealth of information available on Asia at **www.tuttlepublishing.com.**

Published by Tuttle Publishing, an imprint of Periplus Editions (HK) Ltd.

www.tuttlepublishing.com

Copyright © 2024 Toshinori Ohmori and Alexander Bennett

ISBN: 978-4-8053-1765-5

Distributed by:

Japan
Tuttle Publishing
Yaekari Building 3rd Floor
5-4-12 Osaki Shinagawa-ku, Tokyo 141 0032
Tel: (81) 3 5437-0171
Fax: (81) 3 5437-0755
sales@tuttle.co.jp
www.tuttle.co.jp

North America, Latin America & Europe
Tuttle Publishing
364 Innovation Drive
North Clarendon, VT 05759-9436 U.S.A.
Tel: 1 (802) 773-8930
Fax: 1 (802) 773-6993
info@tuttlepublishing.com
www.tuttlepublishing.com

Asia Pacific
Berkeley Books Pte. Ltd.
3 Kallang Sector #04-01, Singapore 349278
Tel: (65) 6741-2178
Fax: (65) 6741-2179
inquiries@periplus.com.sg
www.tuttlepublishing.com

27 26 25 24   5 4 3 2 1   2407VP
Printed in Malaysia

Contents

The History and Spirit of OSU – The Universal Language of Fighters

On August 3, 2016, the International Olympic Committee (IOC) approved 18 additional events in five sports for inclusion in the 2020 Olympic Games to be held in Tokyo. Four of the five were Western sports. Karate was the only Asian sport to be added to the list.

The World Karate Federation (WKF), an IOC recognized body, is responsible for overseeing karate in all five continents, and currently administers 200 national and regional karate federations. The WKF's slogan for the first Olympic Games was "SAY OSS! FOR KARATE." OSU* (pronounced as *oss*) has clearly become a universal calling sign in the karate world.

In June 2014, when karate was lobbying for selection as an official sport for the Tokyo Olympics, Japan's Chief Cabinet Secretary at the time, Suga Yoshihide, was appointed chairman of the Parliamentary

Union for the Promotion of Karatedo. While a student at Hosei University, Suga served as vice-captain of the Gōjū-ryū Karate Club and reached the rank of 2nd Dan black belt. In September 2020, Suga became the 99th Prime Minister of Japan. He was in office when the Olympic Games were finally held in 2021 after a delay due to the pandemic. The captain of Suga's karate club from his student days said in an interview, "Suga always used to communicate with OSU." It seems that the PM of Japan was a quintessential OSU man.

OSU also appears in the lyrics of *KARATE*, a song released in February 2016 by the Japanese female metal dance unit, Babymetal. Their second album, *Metal Resistance*, which includes the song *KARATE*, was released simultaneously worldwide on April 1, 2016, and ranked 39th on the US Billboard magazine's overall album chart. It was the first time in 53 years, and only the second time in history, that a Japanese artist managed to reach the top 40. The first was Kyu Sakamoto's 1963 song, *Sukiyaki*. Whenever Paul McCartney comes to Japan for a performance, he consistently welcomes his fans with "OSU" at both the airport and the concert locations. It appears that the image of karate, "OSU," and Japan are deeply interconnected.[1]

An acquaintance of mine visited the United Arab Emirates in August 2012. He told me that in the UAE, Brazilian Jiu-Jitsu officials also frequently exchange OSUs with each other. I was surprised to learn from another colleague that when the well-known judoka Saitō Hitoshi passed away in January 2015, a message of condolence sent by the Singapore judo community included the word OSU.[2] The reason for my surprise is because the term is not typically used by *jūjutsu* or judo practitioners in Japan.

It is fascinating to see how the use of OSU has expanded beyond karate and into other martial arts like judo, aikido, Brazilian Jiu-Jitsu, kickboxing, and mixed martial arts (MMA) . OSU, having

1 *Nikkan Sports*, May 16, 2017.
2 1961–2015 Japanese judoka who won gold medals at the 1984 LA Olympics and the 1988 Seoul Olympic Games in the +95kg division.

been embraced in almost 200 countries and territories, is possibly the most widely spoken Japanese word around the world. Serving various purposes such as a greeting, a response, or a statement of determination, OSU has turned into a global emblem of the discipline and respect associated with martial arts. Interestingly, in Okinawa, where karate originated, the term OSU is almost unknown. At least, it is rarely heard.

The prevalent adoption of OSU sparks fascinating inquiries: What are its roots, and how did it ascend to such universal prominence? Moreover, what does it truly represent? After extensive research into historical texts and engaging with many authorities on Japanese martial arts, I am excited to reveal an authentic narrative of OSU. Within the pages of this conclusive book, I will explore the differing viewpoints regarding OSU and delve into the etymology of this enigmatic term. This work will settle ongoing discussions on the origins and meaning of once and for all.

*Note From the Author and Translator

Should the *kanji* 押忍 be romanized as OSU or OSS? The world seems to be split on this and you will find both versions depending on the organization. In this book, it will be written as OSU (capitals). This will also be used to refer to the term as used at Takushoku University. The slang term, commonly used as an informal greeting unspecific to martial arts and typically written in *hiragana* as おす or in *katakana* as オス, will be presented as *osu* (in lower case italics).

Other Japanese words and expressions have been divided into their most logical components to assist reading and pronunciation. Japanese terms have been romanized according to the Hepburn system and italicized, and macrons have been used to approximate long vowel sounds. Japanese names are listed in the conventional Japanese order with the surname first. Japanese words found in most standard English dictionaries and names of the modern budo disciplines such as karate and judo are treated as Anglicized words or proper nouns.

The Origins of OSU

The evolution of any language is to be expected with shifting values and attitudes of the people who use it. New words are constantly created, and old ones are lost or take on new meaning. To give an example of this phenomenon in Japanese, the second-person pronoun *kisama* (= honorable highness) was used by samurai until the end of the Muromachi period (1336–1573) as a polite way for addressing people of equal or superior rank. However, in the Edo period (1603–1868), it lost its respectful implications and became a rather vulgar term used by commoners (*kisama* = pal). After its adoption by the modern military, it evolved into a term of affection and familiarity for individuals of the same or lower rank. Over time, it devolved into a derogatory insult (*kisama* = asshole). Nowadays, one would never use this word in Japan unless seeking a confrontation! This illustrates how the use and meaning of words can shift over time.

Simple pleasantries are no different in this sense and are particularly prone to truncation. Sociolinguist Kuramochi Masuko makes the following observations about the common practice of abbreviating words in the Japanese language.

> "The shortening of _ohayō gozaimasu_ (good morning) to _osu_ is a sign of familiarity and camaraderie... But, what drives us to condense words? There are two main motivations for doing this: The first is our inclination to avoid making more effort than necessary. The other is because it can be a more effective means of communication... The communicator, however, must be confident that his or her intentions will be understood even when departing from the fundamental form of a word."[1]

It is fitting for the theme of this book that Kuramochi uses the example of _ohayō gozaimasu_.

The Usual Kind of "_Osu_" in Japan

Elementary school children in Japan formally greet their teachers in the morning with a hearty _ohayō gozaimasu_ (good morning) but abbreviate the term to _ohayō_ (g'morning) when acknowledging classmates. Further compression to _ohayassu_, _oosu_ and _osu_ (mornin') is a custom not confined to a particular organization or region. It occurs naturally throughout Japan, and has done for some time.

Osu as a greeting has been widely used between males in Japan since the late nineteenth century. It is a masculine pattern of speech rarely used by women. You will hear it shouted by boys when they

---

1 Kuramochi Masuko, "Aisatsu Kotoba no Henka" in _Meikai Nihongo_, No. 18, Nov. 2013, pp. 269-270.

arrive at school in the morning, when they see each other in the corridor during recess, after school in clubrooms, on the sports field or in the gym.

Osu is never used, however, to greet teachers or senior students. It is directed at classmates or those in a younger age group due to its off-the-cuff tone. Although usage is not necessarily limited to the morning time, is a shortened version of the polite salutation of *ohayō gozaimasu*.

Karate's OSU

First, it should be pointed out that not all karate styles or schools use OSU, but many do. In contrast to this standard usage, OSU (or OSS), although also a basic greeting in the karate world, has many other meanings as well. In addition to being a surrogate salutation for morning, afternoon, and evening greetings—*ohayō gozaimasu*, *konnichi wa*, and *konban wa* respectively—OSU is also uttered as a response when your name is called, when saying goodbye, good-night, *itadakimasu* (before partaking in a meal) and *gochisō-sama* (after partaking) ...

The karateka always responds with a vigorous OSU when addressed by a superior. In this case, it is not bad-mannered. Far from it. Instead, it is the expected comeback. Put differently, the versatile OSU is used to convey a range of emotions and responses, including agreement, disagreement, perplexity, surprise, and virtually any other sentiment, all while the speaker subtly alters their facial expressions, gestures, and vocal tone to suit the context.

In the context of karate, OSU is often transcribed with the two *kanji* ideograms 押忍 (literally "push" + "persevere"). There are three different writing systems in Japanese: *kanji*, *katakana* and *hiragana*, and OSU can be written respectively as 押忍, オス, or おす. The last two can also refer to the shortened form of *ohayō gozaimasu*, but the *kanji* rendition is the vernacular of karate.

To avoid confusion in this book, the usual non-karate type of greeting will be written as **_osu_**, and the karate-specific _kanji_ term as **OSU**. Please note that **OSS** is the same, and both spellings are seen martial arts circles outside Japan.

Now then, why did karateka start employing OSU as a greeting, and as a multifarious response to indicate one's intentions vis-à-vis almost everything?

Japanese society is traditionally based on a strict hierarchical structure influenced by Confucian thought. As such, the Japanese language is multi-layered and complicated. It employs all manner of confusing honorific terms to differentiate social rank and levels of intimacy. There are special words and grammatical forms that express various levels of respectful, humble, polite, and even gender-specific speech.

From the feudal era, those lower down in the social pyramid refrained from speaking with familiarity to those of a higher station. That would be immensely impolite. In fact, where inferiors are concerned, the less said the better. Best seen but not heard…

As such, minions and social inferiors wee known to shorten communications into a quiet, acquiescent "_osssu_" accompanied by a humble nod of deference in order to not be thought of as insolent by their superiors. This represented no word in particular, but was more a whisper of subservience. It is not related to karate's OSU.

Osu is commonly described as "A greeting used mainly by practitioners of martial arts such as karate, kendo and judo. It is a simplified form of 'good morning'." Such definitions miss the point entirely and were likely contrived by people with no martial arts experience. As mentioned above, the use of OSU in karate is most certainly not limited to greetings. Furthermore, in kendo and judo _osu_ may be heard as an informal greeting, but rarely if ever will you hear OSU in the karate sense.

What about outside Japan? In Germany, France, the UK, Italy, USA, Russia, Spain, Portugal, Brazil, etc., a search for OSU (OSS) on the Internet reveals that many people are curious about its meaning and origins. "What does OSU mean?" "Why do we say OSU in karate?" Most forthcoming answers are simplistic definitions taken from translations of Japanese websites.

What about academic definitions? There are four Japanese universities with budo (martial arts) departments: International Budo University, Kokushikan University, Nippon Sport Science University, and Tokai University. Also, the Japanese Academy of Budo is a scholastic society in which members conduct research into Japanese martial arts. So far, however, nobody in any of these institutions has conducted a rigorous investigation of OSU.

Internet and research institutes aside, how is OSU defined in some of Japan's better-known dictionaries? In the seventh edition of the *Kōjien*, the king of dictionaries in Japan, two meanings are given in the entry for *Osu*: 1. "A salutation used by men towards subordinates or equals." 2. "A greeting proffered by lowerclassmen to upperclassmen in athletic clubs." The first is *osu*, and the second is loosely referring to OSU. It is a highly insufficient entry, and somewhat misleading. Despite OSU being arguably the most frequently used Japanese word in the world, to this day there is no satisfactory definition to be found in dictionaries.

Another burning question: why is 押忍 read as OSU? On its own, the first *kanji* 押 can be read as *o* and means "to push." However, 忍 (*nin, shino(-bu)* = conceal, endure) is not normally pronounced as *su*. By any normal conventions, the combination of these two *kanji* would never be read as OSU. Why, then, did it become recognized as such, to the extent that the *kanji* is immediately generated by Japanese computers when O-S-U is typed in? Is karate really that influential? It is indeed a mysterious word!

OSU's Etymology

There are four main theories in circulation about the etymology of OSU. I will outline them from here.

(1) The Greater-Japan Budo Vocational School Hypothesis

Riding a wave of nationalism after the outbreak of the Sino-Japanese War in 1894, the people of Japan were inspired to take up the traditional martial arts (*bujutsu* or *budō*). The Dai-Nippon Butoku-kai (Greater-Japan Martial Virtue Society, hereafter referred to as Butokukai) was founded in 1895 as an organization dedicated to promoting and persevering Japan's traditional martial culture. By 1909, Butokukai membership had grown to 1.5 million, and at its peak it had over 3 million members.

In 1912, the Butokukai founded the Greater-Japan Martial Arts Vocational School (Dai-Nippon Butokukai Bujutsu Senmon Gakkō) in Kyoto to train instructors ready to go forth and teach *bujutsu* in the nation's schools as Physical Education. In 1919, its name was changed to Budō Senmon Gakkō (usually abbreviated to Busen). Elite kendo, judo and naginata students (not karate) from all over Japan were selected to undertake an intensive course of training and education. Apparently, *osu* was a ubiquitous salutation popular among the students there. *Kendō Nippon* magazine published an interesting article which explains usage at Busen:

> "According to Saiki Tarō,[2] the popular student word *osu* originated in Busen, and derives from *ohayō gozaimasu*, which became *ohassu*, and finally *osu*. Nowadays, juniors use the word *osu* to their seniors, but this is a [rude] misnomer and was only supposed to be said by seniors to their juniors."[3]

2 Busen class of 1938, kendo Hanshi 9th Dan.
3 *Kendo Nippon*, December 1991, p. 48

The front gate to the Butokuden. This dojo still stands in Kyoto today, and was built in 1899 as the headquarters of the Dai-Nippon Butokukai (logo above) a martial arts organization founded in 1895 to preserve and promote traditional budo (martial ways). It played a key role in standardizing martial arts training and elevating the status of budo within Japanese society. The organization was supported by the government and was instrumental in the modernization and systematization of various disciplines, including judo, kendo, kyudo, and naginata.

According to his testimony, the kind of *osu* used in the legendary Busen school was simply the shortened form of *ohayō gozaimasu* that was already used throughout the country. As this article in *Kendō Nippon* is one of only a few to be found that explicitly discusses the term, it solidified the notion that OSU used by martial artists was invented at Busen. Busen's *osu* was then construed, rather confusingly, as the same OSU as that used in karate. Although Busen was an influential specialist school which focused on nurturing kendo, judo, and naginata teachers, there is absolutely no connection between their *osu* and the OSU used in karate today. Again, OSU is not a part of the kendo and judo lexicon in Japan. Busen myth, busted!

(2) Naval Academy Hypothesis
Another theory suggests that OSU was used among the students of the Naval Academy[4] in Etajima, Hiroshima Prefecture, and that this is the true origin of the word.

When I investigated this possibility, I found that NA cadets certainly had idiosyncratic speech patterns. The words *kisama* (informal "you") and *ore* (informal "me") were used among peers and to juniors. The formal terms *kyōkan* (professor) and *senpai* (senior) were used for instructors and upperclassmen, and the very polite *watashi* (formal "me") when referring to the self. I could not, however, find any reference to OSU.

Although well into their nineties now, surviving graduates still keep in touch with each other, and even hold reunions[5]. Some of them have personal blogs online. I was fortunate to be able to correspond with two graduates and ask them directly.

"Hell no! *Osu* was never said at the Naval Academy.

---

4 An educational institution that operated from 1876 to 1945 to train officers of the Imperial Japanese Navy.
5 As of 2013.

Discipline was incredibly strict there. We would never use such vulgar language." (Kajimoto Mitsuyoshi, 76th cohort).

"There's no way we No. 3s would say that! (The most senior students were called No.1s, then followed by No.2s, No.3s and No.4s). I don't remember us ever saying *osu* to each other." (Hosoki Gorō, 77th cohort).

Thus, it is thus highly unlikely that *osu*, let alone OSU, was ever used at the Naval Academy. The Academy's gentlemanly education was influenced by Major Archibald Lucius Douglas at the beginning of the Meiji period, and was modeled on that of the Royal Naval College and the British public school system. Uttering such a colloquial term as *osu* was unthinkable in this environment.

Although there is no evidence suggesting *osu* was used at the elite Naval Academy, it was, however, heard among Naval Flight School reserve students[6]. Kageyama Keiichi joined the Tsuchiura Naval Air Squadron in September 1943 as a reserve cadet in the Naval Flying Corps. He stated the following:

"We used to greet each other in the morning with a hearty *osu*, starting with the first person we met. Actually, we would say *osu* when we met somebody for the first time that day, even if it wasn't the morning. It was basically our way of saying hello to each other. It comes from *ohayō gozaimasu* and was usually reserved for peers or to address the lower ranks. When a senior cadet encountered a junior, he would simply say *osu* or *ohayō*, and of course would not

6 These were individuals who possessed naval certification and were summoned for military duty during wartime, but otherwise worked as officers in the civilian maritime sector.

salute. When the junior officer was addressed, he would hurriedly salute and respond in kind. But a second lieutenant would never say *osu* to a first lieutenant. He might say it to someone he knew well, but would usually just salute."[7]

Osu was also used by the Marines.[8] Kobayashi Takahiro joined the Yokosuka Marines in June 1938.

"In the Navy, we would say *ohayō* in the morning. To superiors it was *ohayō gozaimasu*. I don't know when shortening it to *osu* became acceptable among equals, but woe be the one who said it to a superior. There would be serious consequences for being a 'cheeky bastard!'

In other words, *osu* was reserved for equals or inferiors. At the same time, it was only used in the morning.[9] The following description of *osu* can be found in the popular novel *Kaigun* (Navy) by Iwata Toyo'o (also made into a film).

"On a battleship, *ohayō gozaimasu* was always shortened to *osu*. Except to a higher ranking officer, of course. You would be scolded for insolence if you dared say such a familiar greeting to a superior."[10]

The Imperial Japanese Navy was an organization of many divisions, and the rules surrounding the use of *osu* varied considerably. As a recap, the Naval Academy forbade the use of *osu*. However,

7 Kageyama Keiichi, *Gakuto Shutsujin Yomoyama Monogatari*, pp 39-40.
8 A land-based unit set up by the Imperial Navy to train new recruits.
9 Kobayashi Takahiro, *Zoku-Kaigun Yomoyama Monogatari*, pp. 226-7.
10 Iwata Toyo'o, *Kaigun*, p. 320.

on warships and in the Naval Air Corps and Marines, *osu* was acceptable as a shortened version of *ohayō gozaimasu*, similar to the practice already prevalent throughout the country.

Testimony – Kanai Kimio, Professor Emeritus at the National Defense Academy

"The Naval Academy was modeled on the aristocratic traditions of the British Royal Navy in order to nurture gentlemen officers. As such, correct language was strictly observed. Abbreviated greetings were forbidden. The Naval Air Corps was primarily concerned with training capable combatants, and the Marines focused on teaching the fundamentals of military education, so language was substantially looser than in the Naval Academy."

Naval Academy myth, busted!

A senior ranked soldier greeting his subordinate with a casual "osu". This is merely an informal greeting that is different to the OSU heard in martial arts today.

(3) The Hagakure Hypothesis

Another fascinating theory regarding the origins of OSU links it to the *Hagakure*, a classical text on bushido written by a samurai of the Saga-Nabeshima clan in the early 1700s. Tashiro Tsuramoto (1678–1748) wrote and compiled the book based on the oral teachings of Yamamoto Jōchō (1659–1719), a former samurai in service of the Nabeshima lords. *Hagakure* is famous for the phrase, "The way of the warrior is to be found in dying."

This principle has gained a notorious reputation in the field of bushido studies, commonly misinterpreted as encouraging warriors to recklessly engage in perilous situations without any heed to the consequences, emulating their forebears' fearless actions during the chaotic Warring States period. Yet, this reading misses the mark. Jōchō initially crafted this axiom as a caution to young samurai who, in the tranquil Tokugawa period, had grown complacent and neglectful, squandering their existence instead of dedicating themselves fully to their lord's service.

According to this theory, young samurai of the Nabeshima domain would boost each other's morale by shouting "*Osu! Osu!*" as they crossed paths in the street. In the *Hagakure* itself, however, NO mention of OSU to be found whatsoever. There are vaguely similar words like *oshi-kudasaru* (押しくださる = polite term for receiving something from a superior) and *shinobi-koi* (忍恋 = concealed love), but no 押忍. I could find no reference to young samurai saying OSU or *oss* to each other at all.

I asked Koike Yoshiaki, Professor Emeritus at Toyo University who has written extensively on the *Hagakure*. He replied that he had never come across such a thing either.

It is clear that this theory is nothing more than a figment of someone's imagination. *Hagakure* was once considered a contentious book in the Nabeshima domain due to its somewhat critical assessment of local officials. Despite being a candid account of how a samurai should live his life, it was never included as a teaching material in the Nabeshima domain school where young warriors were educated. In fact, the book was banned by the clan authorities. It came only out into the open in the early twentieth century when ideas of bushido were being commandeered as an integral part of the modern Japanese identity and nationalism.

The originator(s) of the *Hagakure* hypothesis probably sought to connect OSU with the hardliner bushido ideals espoused in the book to give it an air of authenticity and legitimacy. The association between OSU and *Hagakure* bushido was accepted at face value and never questioned. For those who heard or read about the theory, it was surely plausible due to the sentimental attachment to the values of bushido and militarism during the prewar years. *Hagakure* myth, busted!

Nabeshima domain samurai were rumored to have greeted each other with OSU, but no proof of this practice can be found in the pages of the Hagakure, *the famous book explaining the customs of warriors from this region.*

(4) Takushoku University Hypothesis

After investigating different theories about the origins of OSU, there is no clear evidence to confirm any of the aforementioned hypotheses. However, there is another theory that appears to be more convincing. It posits that Takushoku University, a prestigious institution renowned for its karate and other martial arts programs, is the true source of OSU.

Currently, OSU is mainly heard in Shotokan karate related groups like the Japan Karate Association, and other karate organizations such as Kyokushin Kaikan. They were established by alumni of, or have strong connections with Takushoku University. Through an examination of historical records and first-hand accounts, I have concluded unequivocally that origins of OSU can in fact be attributed to Takushoku University. In the following chapters, I will offer evidence to corroborate this hypothesis, and determine once and for all the genesis and true meaning of 押忍.

A light-hearted illustration of Takudai students energetically waving a banner inscribed with OSU in bold katakana at the top followed by "Kōryō Kondei" a moniker that Takudai students referred to themselves as. "Kōryō" means a hill of autumn leaves, i.e., a school reflected in the autumn leaves, and was an epithet of the university. "Kondei" means "able-bodied youth," and was taken from a system developed by the Japanese Imperial court in Nara during the Nara and early Heian periods for the conscription and regulation of local paramilitary or militia forces. An appropriate translation of the banner would be along the lines of "OSU Takudai stalwarts." ("King" March, 1954)

CHAPTER 2

The OSU Era

Takushoku University (Takudai)

Takushoku University (hereafter abbreviated to Takudai) was founded in 1900 by Prince Katsura Tarō.[1] Destined to become a future prime minister of Japan, he established Takudai with the aim of educating young men who could contribute to the development of Japan's recent colonial acquisition, Taiwan. Takudai was originally called the "Taiwan Association School," and was changed in name to Takushoku University in 1918. Katsura himself served as the second Governor General of Taiwan. The territory was ceded to Japan in 1895 following victory over China in the First Sino-Japanese War.

The *kanji* for Takushoku (拓殖) combines two characters, 拓 (*taku*) and 殖 (*shoku*), which together can have a meaning related to expansion, colonization, or development. 拓 alone means to expand, clear (land), or open up. 殖 refers to increase, multiply, or grow.

---

1 1848–1913. Appointed as the 11th, 13th, and 15th Prime Minister of Japan. Former samurai, military man and politician.

As the name of the school suggests, the main agenda pursued by Takudai before the war was represented by the mottoes *Fukkō Ajia* (Restoring Asia) and *Kaigai Yūhi* (Valiantly Crossing the Seas). The founders saw an urgent need to nurture "salt of the earth" (*chi no shio*) types with "high ideals to promote the liberation and independence of Asian countries, hitherto oppressed and exploited by European colonial powers."

Takudai's educational program of cultivating "salt of the earth" human resources is often paired with the phrase "light of the world" (*yo no hikari*). This is actually quoted from the Gospel of Jesus Christ in the Bible. Why would the words of Christ be incorporated into the educational ideals of Takudai? It was certainly not established as a Christian university. It was undoubtedly due to the influence of Nitobe Inazō.

Nitobe served as the second Academic Supervisor and Chair of Colonial Policy at Takudai from April 1917 to April 1922.[2] Nitobe was also directly involved in the colonial rule of Taiwan as a high-level bureaucrat for the Japanese government, and was largely responsible for invigorating the sugarcane industry there.

Nitobe was a committed Christian (Quaker) and believed that the Gospel taught the importance of setting a righteous example, expunging corruption from the world, and supporting society from the bottom up. Therefore, "*takushoku*" in his mind essentially embodied the spirit of venturing from one's homeland to blaze new trails and cultivate new areas, thereby fostering a thriving social and economic landscape for all people.

Nitobe is most remembered now for his classic book *Bushido: The Soul of Japan*. It was written in English in 1899 (published in 1900) to explain the Japanese mind to Westerners. It has since been translated into more than 30 languages and was largely responsible

---

2 1862–1933. Agricultural economist, educator, and international statesman. Nitobe was an advocate of international peace, and served as the under-secretary of the League of Nations. His portrait once adorned the 5,000-yen banknote.

Katsura Tarō (1848-1913).

Nitobe Inazō (1862-1933).

for making bushido (Way of the samurai) an internationally recognized term. Although the theme of his treatise concerns samurai ideals, it can be considered as one of the first attempts in English to explain in detail the values and customs that permeated Japanese society.

Nitobe authored the book to illustrate that, even without a conventional tradition of "religious education" in Japanese schools, the country's ethical core was derived from warrior code of bushido. He depicted bushido as an amalgamation of Confucian, Buddhist, and Shinto values. Furthermore, he contended that bushido was very similar in many ways to Christianity.

Nitobe's global reputation as an expert on international affairs made his selection as the Academic Advisor of Takudai a suitable choice. Takudai students were ambitious young men who came from various parts of Japan with the aim of venturing out into the wider world. They were united by the common principles and ideals promoted by Takudai, which emphasized nurturing a strong sense of purpose for the betterment of society as a whole.

Professors at Takudai passionately imparted a wide range of patriotic and ethical teachings to their students. Core tenets like *Shitsujitsu-gōken* (Simplicity and Fortitude) and *Gōki-bokutotsu* (Steadfastness and Prudence) exemplify the mentality that the university aimed to cultivate.

"Salt of the earth" idealists to the core, students saw themselves as the personification of "anti-sophistication," and they loathed the hedonism that was starting to take root in Japan in the early part of the twentieth century.

The rough and ready, rollicking nature of Takudai students was a prevailing characteristic of their's from the outset. There is no shortage of stories concerning their rambunctious shenanigans during the Occupation in the immediate postwar years. Dressed in traditional *haori*,[3] *hakama*,[4] and *geta*,[5] they would venture into the Ginza area of Tokyo to prey on unsuspecting Occupation Army soldiers. In shows of seeming kindness, they would offer to escort foreign military personnel back to their quarters only to push them unceremoniously in the moat surrounding the imperial palace. They were referred to as "samurai students," and their alma mater was known locally as "Samurai College."

Despite the school's enterprising backstory, or more accurately because of it, Takudai was condemned by GHQ after Japan's defeat for "training pawns of Japanese militarism." Rumors that the university would be dissolved led to determined efforts by Takudai stakeholders to somehow ensure continued operation. The school managed to avoid outright dissolution by starting afresh and changing its name to Kōryō University. This name was used from November 1945 to October 1952. Takudai graduates were forbidden from playing an active role in overseas ventures, especially in Asia. Notwithstanding, the ideals of "internationalism" and "localism" that the school was founded remained at the crux of its educational policy throughout the postwar period.

The main gate of Takudai, temporarily renamed here as Kōryō University, stands as a historical testament to a brief postwar period when the institution was compelled to change its name to distance itself from associations with Japanese expansionism.

---

3 A type of kimono overcoat worn by men.
4 Traditional split-skirt trousers.
5 Wooden platform clogs

Takudai's OSU

Even though the *kanji* for OSU had not been invented yet, Takudai's employment of the word in the prewar years was already replete with profound implications that far exceeded the informal greeting *osu*. Osamu Tezuka is lauded as the "God of Manga" in Japan. He was a fan of the popular graphic novel "Tank Tankuro" when he was a boy. In 1939, the author of this manga, Sakamoto Gajō traveled to Manchuria (now northeastern China) to visit Japanese personnel stationed in the region. Based on his experiences there, he produced the "Manchurian Construction Labor Service Corps Manga Field Report." One section is titled "OSU!" It depicts Takudai students in Manchuria as witnessed in the flesh by Sakamoto.

> "When we arrived in Yilan, we were greeted by four members of the advance team: Takada, Kaida, Ide, and Fukuda. They were all Takudai students and wore their school uniforms and horned caps. They were also carrying guns. They suddenly shouted 'OSU!' at me so loudly, I was left somewhat startled. It is said that OSU is a greeting unique to Takushoku University students. Apparently, it means 'push,' and is suggestive of positive progress. If you don't push, you won't be able to develop anything new. Push through and prosper. Never a greater greeting have I ever heard…"[6]

After graduating from Takudai in December 1941, Shioda Gōzō,[7] founder of Yōshinkan Aikido, wrote about a reunion he had in Taiwan with Nojima Tōzō (member of the 1936 National Collegiate

6 Sakamoto Gajō, "Manshū Kensetsu Kintō Hoshitai Manga Genchi Hōkoku" (Tairiku Kensetsu-sha, 1939) p. 15.
7 1915–1994. See Chapter 4.

Judo Championship winning team). They were close friends in their Takudai days.

> "Without prior notice, Nojima paid me a surprise visit. Standing on the stairs, I heard someone calling my name and upon looking down, I spotted him standing there. I greeted my long-time friend with a warm OSU and he reciprocated in kind."[8]

Shimada Seitarō was a well-known senior member of the Takudai Judo Club whom Nojiima admired immensely. On September 7, 1937, in Shanghai, Shimada bravely charged towards the enemy lines while dressed in his Takudai uniform and cap, ultimately succumbing to enemy fire. His heroic act earned him widespread recognition with several newspapers and magazines reporting on his death. Later that month, a play in his memory was staged at a theater in Asakusa. Nojima wrote of his impressions after going to see the production.

> "From all appearances, the actor who played the role of Shimada must have done his homework and interviewed quite a few Takudai people. He was dressed in a traditional Japanese *haori* and *hakama* [formal wear for men], and his swagger and manner of speaking resembled that of a genuine Takudai student. I was reassured by his attention to detail. The theater was packed with Takudai students. They all cheered in approval shouting 'Ooosssu!!', 'Jolly good fellow, you're a Takudai student now!' 'Hip-hip hooray!' The applause was deafening."[9]

8 Shioda Gōzō, *Shioda Gōzō no Aikidō Jinsei* (2012), pp.101-102.
9 *Takkon no Kiseki: Takushoku University Judo Club Hyakunen-shi* (2002) p.102.

一五　オス！

依蘭へ着いたら街まで先遣隊員が出迎へてくれた、高田、甲斐田、井出、福田の四君で何れも角帽整服姿の拓大學生だ。鐵砲をかついでゐる。勇ましい、いきなり「オス！」と怒鳴つた、びつくりするやうな大きな聲で「オス！」これは拓大生獨特の挨拶ださうである。オスは「押す」で積極前進を意味するさうな、押せ然らば開かれ、押しの一手で開拓しろと、なるほど千萬言にも勝るうれしい挨拶であつた。

Sakamoto Gajō's "Manchurian Construction Labor Service Corps Manga Field Report" authored in 1939. Takudai students are depicted on the right, Army personnel on the left.

A newspaper article celebrating the publication of Yonemoto Wataru's diary from the war years.

"This diary may become my last will and testament. I hereby write down what I am feeling as a clue to my life for those reading it after my death."

These are the first words written by Takudai student Yonemoto Wataru in his diary from June 1941 to October 1944. He was assigned to a naval aviation unit and was killed in a training accident. In 1976, his younger brother, Hitoshi, discovered his diary and decided to publish it.

"Starting September 11, 1941, a new school year kicks off. I'm set on tackling this term with optimism and giving it my all to snag some top grades. Aiming for an average of 85 or higher, I'm committed to putting in the hard work. My goal is to shape up into someone worthy of respect, fueled by dedication and effort. And I've got to keep reminding myself: believe in your own capabilities. OSU."

Also, Moto'o Yoshida, an alumnus of the Takudai Karate Club, reminisced about his experiences in the club in 1941.

> "All the OSUs (=guys) who went to Numazu for the summer camp lined up in front of me with the clattering of their clogs reverberating across the station platform."[10]

These entries demonstrate how OSU was used at Takudai before and during the war. I was surprised to discover that OSU was not only a verbal exclamation but was also expressed in written form (*hiragana* or *katakana*) at Takudai back then. Nevertheless, I have been unable to find any proof that the *kanji* characters 押忍 were in use at this time. This development was to occur in the future. However, the significance of the word had already become deeply integrated into Takudai's cultural fabric.

Iijima Isamu is a well known figure in Takudai's history both before, during, and after World War II. Those familiar with Iijima and his accomplishments hold him in high esteem, considering him to be a truly exceptional individual.[11]

In the summer of 1942, when he was 20 years old, Iijima dropped out of Takudai to participate in "Greater Asianism," an ideological movement that promoted political and economic unity and cooperation among Asian peoples. After all, this was at the heart of Takudai's educational mission. He joined the Sakamoto Teishintai military unit formed by Sakamoto Ken'ichi. Sakamoto was famous for attacking Makino Nobuaki, Lord Keeper of the Privy Seal of Japan, as a part of the May 15 Incident of 1932. Makino survived, but the attempted coup resulted in the assassination of Prime

---

10 Hiroshi Kinjō, *Gekkan Karatedō* (Monthly Karatedo, Karate Jihō-sha July/August 1956) p.46.
11 1921–2001. Former 2nd Lieutenant in the Army. He established Japan's first security company, Tokubetsu Keibi Hoshō (Tokkei) Co. in 1970, at a time when student activism and labor disputes were raging.

Minister Inukai Tsuyoshi by 11 young naval officers. The incident and light punishments meted out to the perpetrators denoted the rise of militarism in Japan.

In any case, the word OSU can be seen on the left side of the banner at Iijima's send-off party. The fact that the word was used at the time of his departure for war shows how profound the phrase had become as a spiritual prop among Takudai students. It served to boost morale in the most extenuating of circumstances.

In this sense, Takudai's OSU cannot simply be equated with the informal greetings used throughout Japan. It arose from Takudai's mission and its unique academic culture and ideology. It became a symbol of the urgency of the era when it was believed that Japan had to either rival the Western powers, or risk exploitation similar to other Asian nations.

What about after the war? Miyazawa Masayuki, an alumnus of Takudai's wrestling team, worked as a reporter for many years at Japan's first sports newspaper, *Nikkan Sports*. He wrote the following:

> "Before World War II, the Hakone Ekiden (long distance relay race) was the most popular intercollegiate sporting event in Japan. Takudai's Yamamoto Masao was a very successful competitor in this annual event. In January 1953, he arrived on a scooter to cheer on his juniors in his capacity as an alumnus. On the back of his jacket were embroidered the words 'OSU! Takudai'. That sight left a lasting impression on me. When I was a student, OSU was a term of endearment, but it was also meant as a mark of respect to Takudai's sporting opponents."

Iijima Tsuyoshi's farewell party in the summer of 1942. Iijima is seated in the center at the front. OSU can be seen at the top left of the banner.

An article titled "The Revival of our Immortal Karate Club" written by Takahashi Tōru describes the state of Takudai immediately following Japan's defeat.

> "In September 1945, following a lengthy break, I went back to school where I reunited with old classmates now dressed in assorted military uniforms. Everywhere I turned, the air was filled with the sound of people greeting each other, the word 'OSU, OSU, OSU...' resounding all around."[12]

---

12 Takushoku University Reitakukai Karate Club OB Kai, *Takushoku University Reitakukai Karate Club Fifty Years History* (1979) p. 29.

"To a freshman, Suidōbashi and Ikebukuro [near the university] were the streets of hell. No matter which way you turned you were surrounded by seniors. Just saying OSU to everybody who needed to be greeted was no small feat. If you did not acknowledge higher-classmen properly you risked being slapped ten times in the blink of an eye. If your voice was too quiet, you would be admonished, 'OSU (= Oi you!). What's with that pathetic OSU? Too damned quiet. It ain't from the heart. Put your balls into it!'" [13]

Fujito Tatsunobu (17th president of Takushoku University) recalled the time when he was summoned by the head of the infamous Takudai Cheering Squad (*ōendan*) when matriculating there in 1952. (In those days, cheering squads were all male groups known for their stoic discipline and propensity to fight with counterparts from other schools.)

"I was given an ultimatum I could not refuse. 'OSU! (= Oi, you!) Join the Cheering Squad to support our athletes at the Collegiate Sumo Championships in the Kokugikan stadium. You'll stand next to me.'" [14]

Igawa Makoto entered Takudai in 1960. He recalls his experiences when he joined the cheering squad.

"My *senpai* said 'I'm glad to see that a gutsy OSU like you has come to Takudai.' He then took me to the Cheering Squad dormitory. They were drinking

13 *King*, (Dai-Nippon Yūbenkai Kōdansha, March 1954) p.76.
14 Takushoku University Kurenaikai, *Takushoku Daigaku Ōendan-shi: Katari-tsutatete Okitai Koto* (2006) p. 9.

like crazy, and I got completely smashed. One day, I dared to ask my *senpai* a question. 'Why does the Cheering Squad bid Takudai graduates farewell at Yokohama Port when they leave for the Americas?' 'Because the OSUs (=graduates) are going abroad as representatives of Takudai, and so it is only fair that OSU (=we) represent Takudai to wish them bon voyage. Isn't it bloody obvious?!'" [15]

In the Takushoku University Graduation Album of 1950 there is an article explaining OSU usage. The examples used show how multifarious the term is.

"OSU (=you lot) must follow OSU (=your) paths. OSU (=I) will follow OSU own (=my) path. What is OSU?" (*Osu-tachi wa osu-tachi no michi wo susume. Osu wa osu no michi wo susumu. Osu to wa nan zo ya!*)

Founded in 1915, the Takudai Sumo Club boasts a long and illustrious history. The current coach of the team, Masuda Mamoru, told me that when he was an active member of the club more than 30 years ago, he was asked by a graduate from the class of 1926, "Where is OSU's (your) hometown?" (I will have more to say about the Takudai Sumo Club's use of OSU in the following chapter.) The coach of Takudai's Judo Club, Satō Shinichirō, was also once asked by an alumnus, "What is OSU's (your) cohort young man?" It goes on and on…

---

15 Ibid., pp. 130-131.

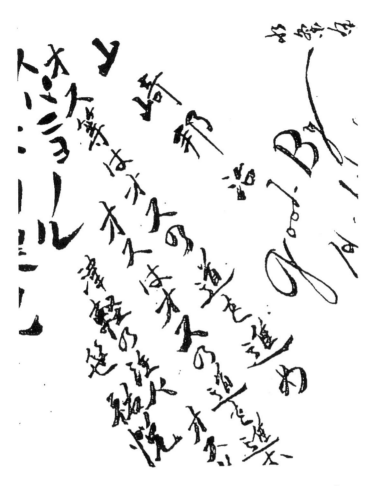

*From the Takushoku University Graduation Album of 1950, the term 'オス'
appears frequently in katakana throughout the inscriptions. The passage
is cryptic, seemingly written in a code-like manner that only fellow Takudai
students could decipher, puzzling to the typical Japanese reader.*

The "OSU Ghetto"

A building known as the Tokyo Gakusei Kaikan[16] once stood in Kudanshita, close to the current location of the Nippon Budokan. Serving as a dormitory, it accommodated students from over sixty universities across the Tokyo metropolitan area. The political atmosphere among students in the postwar period was predominantly left-wing. However, students from Takudai distinguished themselves by resisting this trend, adamantly upholding a conservative right-wing ideology.

Their strong, unyielding stance in favor of these values set them apart, leading the *Mainichi Graphic Weekly* magazine to nickname the area where Takudai students resided as the "OSU Ghetto" in an article written in 1949.

This moniker not only highlighted their ideological uniqueness but also marked a distinct cultural and political enclave within the bustling diversity of Tokyo's academic circles.

> "When you enter the room, you say OSU. When you leave the room, you say OSU. When you greet someone, you say OSU. In all directions of the compass, OSU, OSU, OSU. Life revolves around OSU. The hierarchy separating cohorts is brutal. Freshmen shout 'OSU! I've brought you some water.' 'OSU! I'll go and buy some booze.' OSU is supposedly a derivative of *'oshi'* or push, as used in sumo circles."[17]

Again, I will have more to say on the extremely important sumo connection in the next chapter.

---

16 An autonomous dormitory for male students that existed in the Chiyoda ward of Tokyo from May 1946 to November 1966.
17 Mainichi Club, *Mainichi Newspaper* (June 1, 1949) p. 6.

オス部落

彼らのいう「離飛」の日に備えての空手のけいこだが 離飛とは決して「脱城」という意味ではない と特に強調していた 以上念のため……

「アリヤ シンキンダミノ」とはやまられそうだが角帽をかぶっているため学生であることがわかる「アブナイノ/アブナイノ」とどなりながら歩くのだが 通行人はこの姿を見ただけで いっせいに避けてしまう 彼らにとっては一蹴の暗意を濫用しての外出である

A spotlight on the "OSU ghetto" reveals the tough demeanor of Iakushoku University students through vivid photographs. These students, decked out in Bankara style, are depicted as intense individuals who played hard, trained rigorously, and carried an imposing swagger, often intimidating those unaffiliated with the university. (Mainichi Club, June 1949)

CHAPTER 2

The Karate Novel *Chōsenki*

Asakura Bunjirō graduated from Takushoku University in 1950. He published his karate novel, *Chōsenki*, in 1952. The story is based on the Takudai Karate Club in the aftermath of the war. Asakura himself was a member of the club, albeit for a short time. The author provides an authentic account of how OSU was used in everyday conversation drawing from his own personal encounters with the term.

"Allow me to explain OSU. It is generally believed that the term was originally used by cadets at the old Naval Academy as a morning greeting—a shortening of *ohayō gozaimasu*. Takudai's OSU is a little different. From what I can gather, the word originates from some philosophical notion 'Push and the world will open.'

This viewpoint stems from the tales of individuals who journeyed abroad to develop uncultivated lands. Through their relentless determination and continuous effort to advance their cause, despite seemingly insurmountable odds, they 'pushed forever onwards' to create an environment where flowers bloomed and birds soared. This invaluable lesson of life was imparted to us by our *senpai*.

Following in the footsteps of our esteemed predecessors, students customarily exchanged this term of endearment to fortify their pioneering spirit. It is, however, used in myriad ways. First, it is for greeting others in the morning, afternoon, and evening, as well as saying goodbye, good night, thank you; and

The cover of the karate novel Chōsenki (Challenge Demon), *penned by a graduate of the Takushoku University Karate Club, encapsulates the rigorous spirit and discipline of martial arts woven throughout the story.*

sometimes, you and me. It is also used as 'hey' and just shouting in general. When an higherclassman says 'OSU, do as OSU say. Now, skedaddle. OSU!' The lowerclassman will respond with 'OSU! OSU!' and start running. Anyone within earshot would be completely unaware of what just happened. A rough interpretation might go something like this: 'Listen, do what I tell you to do. If you understand, then you can go now. I'll see you later.' 'Yes, sir, I understand. I'll get right on it. Goodbye...'"[18]

Another example,

"OSU (you lot), get OSU (your asses) over here. I'll lend OSU (you) a karate uniform so you can learn how to put it on... Hey! Never say YES. Always reply with OSU."[19]

In another article written by Asakura Bunjirō:

"Nowadays, students everywhere seem to use the OSU greeting, but Takudai is where it all started... It has been commandeered as a simple greeting from such sentiments as 'No matter how tough things are, if you show fortitude and push through, you will surely see the light.' So, OSU is a fine philosophical paradigm. It invokes the stirring cries of Takudai grads of generations gone by singing the school anthem, 'There is no discrimination where I stand, based on color, race, or birth land!' Takudai students

18 Asakura Bunjirō, *Chōsenki*, (Fuji Shobō, 1952) pp. 105-106.
19 Ibid., pp. 32-3.

started and ended their days with OSU. Everything from good morning, goodbye, to you and me… OSU covers it all. OSU and OSU, then OSU again. OSU! Such a deliciously omnipotent term for any occasion."[20]

In his book, Shōji Hiroshi[21]—alumnus of the Takudai Karate Club and later a master instructor of the Japan Karate Association—writes about his memories in the early 1950s. Even handing over a love letter warranted a spirited OSU.

"One morning, S waited for her at the back gate with a note in his hand. He was a pure-hearted lad. When he spotted her coming, he ran up to greet her. 'Here… OSU!' He handed her the note and ran off again. She must have been a friendly lass because she didn't dismiss his advances. I often laugh at how everything is expressed with OSU. Still, I had no idea that it could come in useful when handing over a love letter."[22]

The Takudai OSU carries a weight of respect and appreciation that transcends its simple utterance. It's a nod to the dedication behind a task accomplished, a bow to the effort and prowess of one's adversaries. Far more than a mere acknowledgment, it serves as a heartfelt salute to the competitive spirit and fair play that define true sportsmanship. This expression of esteem finds its way into various aspects of life, echoing the principles of honor, admiration, and solemnity, even as far as the domain of youthful, bashful romance.

---

20 *King*, Op. Cit., p. 93.
21 1931–2003, winner of the Kata Division in the 1st All Japan Student Karate Championships.
22 Shōji Hiroshi, *Karate e no Michi* (Fukushodō, 1976) p. 107.

Column 1: "OSU" Prohibition Declared by Kyoto Prefectural Police Force

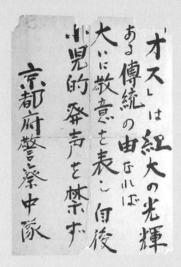

Official notification from the Kyoto Police top brass imploring their officers not to copy Takudai students by saying OSU.

On June 28, 1948, the Fukui Earthquake struck the Hokuriku and northern Kinki region of Japan. It was a powerful earthquake that devastated Fukui City as it was recovering from the ravages of war. The magnitude of the earthquake was 7.1 on the Richter scale, making it the third largest earthquake in the postwar era after the Great East Japan Earthquake (2011) and the Great Hanshin-Awaji Earthquake (1995).

At that time, Fukui City's central region was densely populated, and many buildings collapsed. Over 30 students from Takushoku University (temporarily renamed Kōryō University) went to the area as volunteers to aid the affected people. The relief team stayed at the city hall alongside police officers sent from Kyoto. Together they cleared debris and assisted in the retrieval of victims' bodies. The locals expressed their gratitude towards the students for their assistance, and the mayor of Fukui City bestowed upon them a letter of recognition.

The police and students had a strong relationship, although the students' habit of calling everything OSU was unfamiliar to the police. Soon, the police began adopting this slang from Takudai, much to the annoyance of their higher-ups. Ultimately, they were explicitly instructed not to use OSU in their communications.

CHAPTER 3

The Birth of OSU (押忍)

The Rise of OSU in Postwar Japan

So far in this investigation I have focused on the rise of OSU at Takushoku University. Although OSU was prevalent throughout the prewar years, and embodied a deep and meaningful philosophy, it did not yet have accompanying *kanji*. So, when and how did 押 + 忍 = OSU come into existence?

On August 30, 1945, Supreme Commander of the Allied Powers (SCAP) Douglas MacArthur landed at the Naval Air Facility in Atsugi. MacArthur set up his headquarters in the famous Daiichi Seimei Kan building (currently the DN Tower 21) facing the moat of the Imperial Palace and embarked on a mission to purge Japan of any militaristic and ultra-nationalistic influence.

Fearing a resurgence of nationalistic hostility, SCAP implemented a variety of policies to mitigate any of such tendencies. It disarmed the Imperial Army and Navy, and dismantled Japan's military industry and conglomerates. It forced the country to abandon all ambitions of wielding military power, and did away with the

General Douglas MacArthur, iconic and composed, is captured in a commanding pose with a pipe clenched between his teeth. The pipe, his trademark accessory, adds a touch of contemplative gravitas to his already formidable presence. Although once the enemy, he came to be widely respected in Japan in the postwar period.

authoritarian "Peace Preservation Law" and the infamous Special Higher Police ("Thought Police") that enforced it.

To make Japan a "modern democratic state," SCAP also extended its scalpel to the traditional arts of Japan, which were viewed suspiciously as fostering militaristic sentiment. Even Kabuki performances were banned on the grounds that plays such as "Chūshingura" (Forty-seven Ronin) encouraged revenge and misguided loyalty. They also prohibited the screening of *chanbara* (sword fighting) movies because of the perceived barbarity of wielding *katana* in frenzied death matches.

The "Imperial Rescript on Education" established by the Meiji emperor in 1890 was abolished and the new Basic Education Law was enacted in schools. In addition, the Dai-Nippon Butokukai (Greater Japan Society for Martial Virtue)—the national association created in 1895 to promote traditional martial arts—was dissolved for being a "dangerous militaristic organization," and mainstream budo such as kendo and judo were prohibited.

Of all the universities in Japan, Takudai was subjected to considerable criticism for its role in expansionism. Takudai's philosophy from the days when it was known as the Taiwan Association School was viewed as having been at the vanguard of Japanese colonialism and militarism. Japan's aspirations for Asia, which formed the basis of the university's ideals before the war, were completely rejected and it was even forced to change its name (Kōryō University) in order to continue operating.

I contend that Takudai students conceived the *kanji* characters for OSU (押忍) amid this chastening time for their school. OSU took on a new life that symbolized the rebellious attitude of students at Takudai toward the US-led occupation. It also reflected their fervent aspiration to revitalize Japan from the ruins of war and make it prosperous once again.

CHAPTER 3

The New Spirit of OSU

The following saying was passed down through generations of Takudai students in the postwar period:

> "Endure the unendurable and suffer what is not sufferable. Push when pushed. Push when pulled. This spirit of self-denial is the essence of OSU."

Where did this notion come from? On August 14, 1945, Emperor Hirohito endorsed the Potsdam Declaration during the Imperial Conference and released the "Imperial Rescript of the End of the War," signaling Japan's surrender to the world. That evening, the emperor delivered a speech from the government office within the Imperial Palace. At noon on August 15, NHK Radio, Japan's national broadcaster, aired the emperor's address to the exhausted populace. With this broadcast, the harrowing conflict of unparalleled hardship ultimately concluded. Towards the end of the speech, he said,

> "It is according to the dictates of time and fate that we have resolved to pave the way for a grand peace for all the generations to come by enduring the unendurable and suffering what is not sufferable."

Tokyo and other significant urban areas lay in ruins, ravaged by air raids and firebombing, while reports of atomic bombs devastating Hiroshima and Nagasaki circulated widely. Although a prevailing sense of impending defeat permeated the air, the broadcast definitively conveyed to the Japanese populace that the war had indeed reached its end. Scores of citizens gathered before the Imperial Palace amidst the scorching heat, tears streaming down their faces as they bowed deeply to the ground.

It is rumored that the originator of the phrase "Endure the

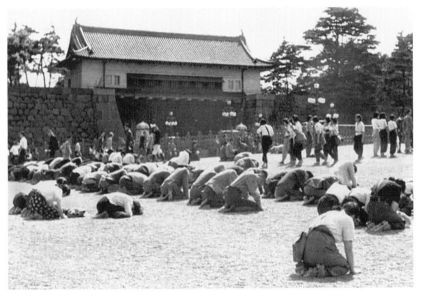

In a poignant moment captured in front of the Imperial Palace, Japanese citizens are seen prostrating in deep reverence and sorrow following Japan's surrender. This powerful image reflects a nation in mourning. The scene symbolizes a critical juncture in Japanese history, marking the end of imperial ambitions and the beginning of a new era of rebuilding and transformation into a new democratic society.

unendurable and suffer what is not sufferable" was Yamamoto Gempō,[1] head priest of Ryūtakuji Temple. Just before the Imperial Conference to deliberate on Japan's impending surrender, Yamamoto told Prime Minister Suzuki Kantarō[2] "We will enter a critical time from now on, so please endure what will be hard to endure, do what is difficult to do. And, take care of yourself."

Although it is commonly believed that this passing comment was the inspiration behind the emperor's message, this assumption is actually wrong. The phrase "*Gyōji-gataki wo gyōji, shinobi-gataki koto wo shinobu*"[3] (endure what is difficult to endure, and suffer what is not sufferable), appears in an ancient Chinese text on Zen Buddhism called the *Keitoku Dentō-roku* ("The Jingde Record of the Transmission of the Lamp") compiled during the Song dynasty.[4]

To "endure" and to "suffer" essentially mean the same thing. This repetition of synonyms was meant to add emphasis to the grit and determination required to survive the anguish and humiliation of defeat. The first line in the Takudai verse introduced above appears to have been taken from the emperor's speech. Furthermore, it is followed by another phrase: "Push when pushed, push when pulled" (押さば押せ、引かば押せ = *Osaba ose, hikaba ose*). This idiom represents the lifeblood of sumo—traditional Japanese wrestling—and finally points us to the true origin of OSU (押忍) as we know it now...

Sumō In'un-kai — The Book of Sumo Secrets

Sumo is many things. It is a martial art. It is a popular form of entertainment enjoyed by millions of spectators on TV six times a year. It is also a ritual ceremony conducted for a bountiful harvest

---

1 1866–1961, Japanese Zen monk, and abbot of Ryūtakuji Temple in Mishima, Shizuoka Prefecture.
2 1868–1948, Japanese naval officer and politician who became the 42nd Prime Minister of Japan.
3 Murakoshi Eiyū, *Gekkan Jūshoku Bessatsu Hōwa Tokushū* (Kōzansha, August 2019) pp. 11–12.
4 960–1127, Chinese Dynasty.

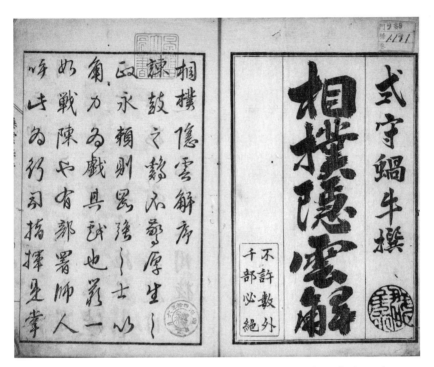

A page from "Sumō In'un-kai," an eighteenth century text that explains the lesser-known aspects of sumo wrestling, including strategies, rituals, and philosophy. This detailed guide provides insights into the techniques and traditions that are integral to the sport but hitherto hidden from the public eye.

(*gokoku-hōjō*) for the "Five Grains."[5] As a form of traditional culture, sumo has played an important role in Japanese society from historical times to the present day. It is widely referred to now as Japan's national sport.

Sumo can be traced back to the mythological age when, according to a vignette in the *Nihon Shoki* (Chronicles of Japan, 720), Nomi-no-Sukune and Taima-no-Kehaya wrestled each other to the death at the request of the emperor. Sukune fatally wounded Kehaya by breaking his ribs with a single kick and his spine with another. While it wasn't anything like contemporary sumo wrestling, Sukune is nonetheless considered the progenitor of sumo.

Fujio Yasutarō, head instructor of the Takudai Judo Club from 1929 to 1930 who later became a prominent politician, wrote the following passage in his book on sumo:

> "Judo is based on the principle of skillfully utilizing the opponent's attack against them. That is to pull when pushed and push when pulled. In sumo, however, the guiding technical principle is push forward when pushed, and push forward when pulled. In other words, to always take the fight to the opponent and never take a step back. This variance in the use of strength and technique between judo and sumo is due to the difference in shape and size of the match area [where the sumo mound is round and much smaller]. In short, the very essence of sumo, its life-force, lies in the act of pushing forward. When I was instructor for the Takudai Judo Club, our university was a national powerhouse in collegiate sumo. Members of the Sumo Club used to say '*o-su*'—the plain form of the verb *oshi-masu* (to push)—to each other instead

---

5 Abundant harvest of grain. The five grains are rice, wheat, millet, beans, and millet.

of hello.[6] I suppose that this was simply reaffirmation of the absolute imperative of pushing in sumo [as opposed to the *osu* as an abbreviated greeting customarily used by other students]."[7]

The book *Sumō In'un-kai* was written in 1793. The author was the legendary Edo period (1603–1868) sumo *gyōji* (referee), Shikimori Inosuke the first. Inosuke retired from adjudicating sumo bouts in the third month of 1793. In the seventh month of that year, he wrote his opus, *Sumō In'un-kai* (Hidden Clouds of Sumo), under the pseudonym Shikimori Kagyū. Being the first book of its kind that delved into the "secrets of sumo," it came as a revelation to both wrestlers and aficionados alike. It contains the following somewhat cryptic sentence:

> "Pushing is the heart of sumo. It is written with the *kanji* character for *shino-bu* (忍 = endure). The spirit of sumo is to win by holding firm. Endure, endure, endure; when pulled, endure; when thrust at, endure; when you are pulled around, endure..."

"Push back when pushed; push forward when pulled; pushing to win is the secret of sumo." This is now a widely known expression in Japan. The path to victory is simply to push onwards come what may. It is the devastating front-on collisions of wrestlers giving no quarter to their opponents on the mound that excites spectators the most. Jumping out of the way at the last moment might result in a win, but will not be seen as being in the true spirit of sumo. It

---

6 The "plain form" of a verb in the Japanese language is also referred to as the "dictionary" or "basic" form. It is the informal present affirmative form of the verb. Connected to this, there are many different verb forms. With the verb in question here, for example, *o-su* is the plain form, *oshi-masu* is the polite form, *osa-nai* and *oshi-masen* are the negative forms, *oshi-ta* and *oshi-mashita* represent the past form, and so on.

7 Fujio Yasutarō, *Budō to shite no Sumō to Kokusaku* (Dai-Nippon Seifū Sha, 1939) pp.163–164.

will be a hollow victory. It is the clash of bodies and wills pushing forward—unstoppable force colliding with immovable object—that people want to see.

But, there is more to this verb "push" than meets the eye. The passage quoted above from *Sumō In'un-kai* expresses the spirit of sumo by replacing the *kanji* for push (押す) with another *kanji* meaning to endure and hold firm (忍す).

The *Sumo Encyclopedia* published by the Japan Sumo Association elaborates on this idea. It explains that the *kanji* for endure (忍 = normally read as *nin* or *shino-bu*) can also read as *o-su*.[8] However, this interpretation is extremely uncommon, and not known by those unfamiliar with sumo. In the world of sumo, however, "endure" is interpreted the same as "push." It is essentially a play on words to give the fundamental action of pushing a philosophical dimension.

Etymology of OSU (押+忍)

So, added together the *kanji* for "push" (押) and "endure" (忍)—both read as *o(-su)* in the context of sumo—serves to add emphasis to the action and the ideal. Philosophically speaking, however, one *o-su* represents yang, and the other *o-su* yin. The two can be thought of as complementary forces that interact to form a dynamic whole. Moreover, in this case *o-su* + *o-su* = OSU.

押 = 陽 → 表 光 火 夏 身体 攻撃 動
O-su = Yang → Front, Light, Fire, Summer, Body, Attack, Action
忍 = 陰 → 裏 闇 水 冬 精神 防御 静
O-su = Yin → Back, Darkness, Water, Winter, Mind, Defense, Stillness

Adding 押 + 忍 together, one may get the impression that 押 = O and

---

8 Kanezashi Motoi, *Sumō Daijiten* (Gendai Shokan, 2002) p. 51.

忍 = *SU* (押忍). The truth is, however, 忍 has no such reading as *SU*. In other words, it is an *ateji*—a *kanji* used to phonetically represent native or borrowed words with less regard to the true reading of the characters. Pairing the two *kanji* creates a sort of linguistic pun that blends the concepts of "push" and "endure" into a single expression pronounced as OSU (OSS).

"Push when pushed; push when pulled; pushing to win is the essence of sumo." This phrase expresses the physical core of sumo. On the other hand, "Endure when pushed; endure when pulled; enduring for victory is the essence of sumo" represents the spiritual dimension of sumo. Thus, "when pushed, hold firm or persevere" (押 + 忍) is an expression encompassing both the physical and spiritual aspects of mastery.

Kasagiyama Katsuichi (1911-71), a student at Waseda University, led a double life as a professional sumo wrestler, drawing considerable attention from the media for his insights into sumo. Given the societal status attributed to college students at the time, simultaneously attending university and engaging in a professional sumo career was unprecedented. He penned many books over his career, and wrote the following observation in one of them:

> "The secret of sumo is to endure (忍す = *o-su*) when pushed, push (押す = *o-su*) when pulled, push and endure (おす = *o-su*, in *hiragana* not *kanji*, so can be interpreted both ways) to attain victory. This means when the opponent pushes, hold firm and take it. It means to be patient. When pushed, push back. If you can't push back, be patient and hold your ground. Next, as soon as the opponent starts going back, follow through and push forward. In this way, pushing through to win is to hold, endure, patiently stand your ground, and then push forward for victory. The word '*o-su*' (usually understood as simply "to push") is a com-

bination of the two meanings of physically ramming the opponent and holding strong while enduring their attacks. This is true sumo. This is the spirit of sumo."[9]

This excerpt eloquently captures the heart of the sumo mindset, and is frequently cited today as the epitome of combat in traditional Japanese wrestling.

Ichinoya, the first sumo wrestler to graduate from a national university and the manager of the professional Takasagoya stable, continues to explore the physical aspects of sumo. He made the following post on his stable's blog:[10]

> "Endure when pushed; push when the opponent pulls; pushing through to win is the quintessence of sumo. *O-su* (押す=push) and *o-su* (忍す=endure) represent the core of sumo's physical and mental skill. 'Push and endure' (OSU) is communicated in karate as well, and surely exemplifies the supreme teaching of budo."[11]

There is a well-known TV celebrity in Japan by the name of Oshizaka Shinobu (押阪 忍). In his book he states:

> "There is a wonderful teaching in sumo. 'Courtesy begins and ends with a bow of respect.' There is another saying, 'Endure when pushed; push when pulled...' That's where the word OSU comes from. It's not exactly the same as my name, but it's close enough...."[12]

---

9 Kasagiyama Katsuichi, *Sumō* (Ōbunsha, 1950) pp. 184–5.
10 1960–, Physics graduate of the University of the Ryukyus, former oldest active sumo wrestler. He is now in charge of sumo in the *Budo Monthly* magazine published by the Nippon Budokan.
11 *Hyper Takasago-beya*, June 29, 2012.
12 Oshizaka Shinobu, *Kotoba no Takarabako* (PHP Research Institute, 2007) pp.167–8.

Oshizaka Shinobu is not his stage name. It is pure coincidence that it contains the same two *kanji* characters as OSU. As a TV personality, Oshizaka is known to most people over 50 years of age in Japan. Having been born in 1935, he is Japan's oldest active announcer and still has a regular television show. Oshizaka almost gave up college due to his family's financial woes, but through the kindness of sumo stablemaster Dewanoumi Oyakata, a close friend of Oshizaka's father from their elementary school, he was able to continue his studies while residing in the

TV talent Oshizaka Shinobu has captivated audiences with his vibrant personality for longer than anybody else in Japan's showbiz world.

Dewanoumi stable. On April 7, 2016, I was able to speak directly with Mr. Oshizaka.

"Although I didn't train in sumo, I woke up at 5:00 a.m. every morning to scrub the corridors and stairs with the new apprentices. After that, I would attend classes and then return to a long list of jobs to do such as cleaning the garden and heating the bath for the senior wrestlers. Luckily, my childhood experience with household chores enabled me to handle these tasks effortlessly.

At the time, there was a scroll displayed on the wall of the stable. It had the *kanji* characters 'Endure When Pushed' (押さば忍せ = *osaba ose*) brushed on it. I understood it to mean that if your opponent drives into you, be patient and hold your ground, bite down and push back. Take it and persevere. Nobody explained the phrase's meaning to me. I just naturally came to understand it by being in that environment. It became a part of me. Years later, when I learned about the karate greeting OSU, I naturally assumed that it came from *osaba ose*...

The still highly popular "Sumo Digest" show, which first premiered on TV in 1959, hired me as its initial announcer. My boss figured I must know a bit about sumo having lived in a stable...

The Oshizaka family traces its roots to Prince Oshi-zaka-no-Hikohito-no-Oe, first son of Emperor Bintatsu of the Asuka period (592-710). I was the youngest of five children. My father was rather short-tempered, so perhaps he named me 'Shinobu' to remind himself to endure and not to get too hot under the collar. I was not comfortable with the name Shinobu as a child as it was more common for girls than boys! One day I was talking to a Buddhist priest. He commented 'Shinobu is such a good name. It has a gentle feeling.' I suppose it seems kind, especially considering the bottom part of the *kanji* (忍) is *kokoro* (心 = heart). The top half is 刃 (*yaiba* = blade), so there is an element of toughness to it as well...

Ever since then, my name has empowered me with courage to endure, and also to persevere even in the toughest of times as if my heart wielded a sword. 'Endure when pushed...' Never give up. I believe this mindset applies to life as well, and I truly appreciate this turn of phrase. Having lived with the principle of OSU for more than 80 years now, it is an integral part of my being...."

OSU ≠ 'Oshi-Shinobu'

Kanji are logographic characters originating in ancient Chinese script. They are a key part of the Japanese writing system alongside the syllabic scripts *hiragana* and *katakana*. It is said that there are over 100,000 characters in China, but Japan never imported all of them. The Japanese National Curriculum designates the *kanji* children must learn in compulsory education (elementary and junior high schools). These are referred to as the "Jōyō Kanji" and total 2136 characters.

In Japan, *kanji* can be read in two ways: *on'yomi* and *kun'yomi*. *On'yomi*, or "sound-based reading," refers to the modern Japanese approximation of the original Chinese pronunciation when it was first introduced into Japan. On the other hand, *kun'yomi*, or "meaning reading," is a native Japanese reading based on the pronunciation of Japanese words that are similar in meaning to the Chinese characters. Just like with *on'yomi*, there can be several *kun'yomi* readings for the same *kanji*.

For example, the word 堪忍 (*kan-nin* = patient endurance, or, to abide) is made up of the two characters 堪 + 忍. The *on'yomi* for 堪 is *kan*, and its *kun'yomi* reading is *tae*(*-ru*). For 忍, the *on'yomi* is *nin*, and the *kun'yomi* is *shino*(*-bu*). Therefore, the *on'yomi* reading for both *kanji* together becomes *kan-nin*. The *kun'yomi* is *tae-shino*(*-bu*).

What about 押忍 then? The *on'yomi* for 押 is *ou*, and the *kun'yomi* is *o*(*-su* or *-saeru*). If OSU (押忍) was originally a Chinese word that made had its way into the Japanese lexicon, it could theoretically be read as *ou-nin*, with a *kun'yomi* of *oshi-shino*(*-bu*). But, OSU was never a Chinese word to begin with. It is a phonetic *ateji* creation of postwar Japan. Therefore, the common misconception

63

山 置 笠　（力角大本日大）

Kasagiyama Katsuichi (1911- 1971) was a sumo wrestler from Ikoma District, Nara Prefecture. His real name was Nakamura Kanji. He belonged to the Dewanoumi stable while studying at Waseda University and the highest rank he reached was Sekiwake.

in Japan that OSU stems from an existent verb *oshi-shinobu* is simply untrue.

When a Japanese person is asked if they know the meaning of OSU, they will usually say, "Ah, yes. It is to *oshi-shinobu*" as if there is such a word in the Japanese language. It is a concoction that came after the advent of OSU. Although *oshi-shinobu* would literally mean "push through and endure," it is incorrect Japanese usage.

This contrived verb was probably disseminated by Japanese karate aficionados and authorities via the Internet, and has subsequently spread around the world. It is perhaps an easy mistake to make, but this is not how the etymology of OSU, or its meaning came about. The opposite is true.

If somebody was to ask how to write the *kanji* for OSU, one might well answer "with the same characters as *oshi* (押し) plus *shinobu* (忍ぶ)..." but it does not have the same nuances. People who explain OSU as *oshi-shinobu,* and there are many, are missing the point.

In any case, we can conclude that origins of OSU can be traced to the sumo phrase *osaba ose* (押さば忍せ)—***when pushed, endure.*** However, *osaba ose* only represents the sumo ideal of holding one's ground when attacked from the front and persevering to eventually push through for victory. It does not capture the full meaning of OSU.

Historical accounts reveal that, during the prewar era, members of the Takudai Sumo Club epitomized the ideals of sumo through the term "push" (*o-su*), adopting it as a unique form of salutation. More crucially, they considered this term as the essence of the "Takudai spirit," signifying a mantra of relentless progression and breakthrough, encapsulated in mottoes like "advance relentlessly and paths will unveil themselves" and "forge ahead to trailblaze." For the students of Takudai, "pushing" meant more than a mere physical act; it represented bonds of fellowship, integrity, motivation, manifesting as a fervent declaration of perseverance. Takudai University was established with the ambition of cultivating a pioneering ethos among its students, preparing them to spearhead Japan's imperial ambitions. OSU came to capture this.

Japan was forced to make major changes to its national policy, as dictated by the Imperial Rescript released after the war. The Rescript called for enduring unbearable circumstances and tolerating the intolerable, signifying a new era in which perseverance and endurance were crucial as Japanese got back on the horse, so to speak.

To Takudai students then, OSU came to represent a rebellious spirit in the face of dishonor experienced under the rule of an occupying force. It was inspired by the sumo teaching of *osaba-ose*. Push *o-su* (押す) became endure *o-su* (忍す), and then OSU (押忍).

To clarify, the term "OSU" in *kanji*, symbolized both a rallying cry and an act of defiance, and was created by Takudai students during the postwar period, a time marked by national humiliation. Therefore, understanding the roots of the OSU requires familiarity with the teachings of sumo and the unique culture of Takudai students.

The Oldest OSU

Based on my research of historical documents and eyewitness accounts, it is evident that Takudai students coined the term OSU employing its two *kanji* sometime between 1945 and 1950. As we have seen, OSU had been customarily exchanged among Takudai students before the war. The origin of the word can be traced back to the Takudai Sumo Club and its emphasis on the highest teachings of sumo, as evidenced by the members' habitual use of the term OSU since the 1930s. It connoted the idea of pushing through all adversity, but it was never written as 押忍 until after the war. It is possible that a returning war veteran came up with the idea upon returning to his studies at Takudai, but I cannot verify who was behind this advancement of the term.

Another autograph page from the Takushoku University Graduation Album of 1950. One can see in the center of the page, just under the small initials "SF" the first known instance of OSU being written with the kanji 押忍.

Notwithstanding, OSU was not adopted by Takudai students all at once. Nor did they start using it after the issuance of some kind of directive to do so. It tricked down organically as part of Takudai's culture in club activities, alumni prefectural associations, dormitories, etc. This is why it is impossible to specify precisely who came up with it in the first place.

The oldest recorded OSU as 押忍 that I have been able to find is in a collection of letters published in the "Takushoku University Graduation Album" of 1950. The characters for 押忍 can be found mixed in with variations written in *hiragana* and *katakana*. I suspect that this must have been a transition period when OSU became firmly established as 押忍. Incidentally, graduation albums from 1945 to 1949 were not published due to postwar distractions and a lack of resources.

Masayuki Miyazawa, a graduate of the Takudai Wrestling Club, recorded,

> "When I was in college (1948–1953), some people on campus used the term OSU with the *kanji* 押忍. Personally, I used OSU (オス in *katakana*), and I have more affinity with this."

Nakamura Fumiyasu, once part of the Takudai Karate Club, recounts the following:

> "In 1948, or there abouts during my junior high years, my teacher informed me that the term OSU was invented at Takudai. I wrote OSU (押忍) at the end of all my letters even before I entered Takudai."

Nakasone Yasuhiro[13] President of Takushoku University from 1967 to 1971 and later Prime Minister of Japan, said in one of his lectures,

"When you come to Takudai, everyone says 'OSU OSU', but just one OSU will suffice. Embrace it everybody. Give a heartfelt OSU."[14]

From the 1940s to the 1980s, OSU was commonly used in Takudai's athletic and cultural clubs by both male and female students. Despite being considered a masculine term, OSU was adopted by all students. I even heard the staff at the Takushoku University Alumni Association office proudly shouting OSU to each other while they worked.

In Japan, there is a custom known as *te-jime* which is performed at the end of a banquet. All attendees stand up together and clap their hands in unison while shouting set phrases. This serves to unite everyone and bring the party to a close. There are various versions. *Ippon-jime* is done by rhythmically clapping ten times (1-2-3, 1-2-3, 1-2-3, 1!). *Sanbon-jime* repeats this sequence three times.

In Takudai, however, it is customary to close ceremonies with *OSU Sanshō* (Three OSU Chant). It starts with the leader loudly shouting "OSU SANSHŌ, YŌI!" (ready). The attendees then shout "YŌISHO!" as everyone assumes a left low block in a karate front stance. Next, the leader shouts "SŌRYAAAAA!" while executing a right mid-level reverse punch followed by a left low block. The attendees perform the same punch/block sequence directly after the leader while shouting "OSSSSSU!" These steps from "SŌRYAAAAA!" onwards are repeated two additional times.

---

13 Japanese politician. Nakasone was the 12th President of Takushoku University and the 71st, 72nd, and 73rd Prime Minister of Japan.
14 *Asahi Journal* (Asahi Shimbun-sha, July 12, 1970) p. 8.

This custom was originally conceived by Nakayama Masatoshi of Takudai's karate club. Now, not only the karate club and cheering squad, but all athletic and cultural clubs and Takudai-related people finish their parties with this ritual. It is even done at weddings and funerals.

The Spread of Karate in Japan

Let us take a step back from OSU now and look at how karate spread within Japan and then the world. This process is also closely linked to the Takudai legacy.

In this historic photograph, Funakoshi Gichin, a pivotal figure in spreading karate in Japan, is captured in a moment of intense focus as he practices on a makiwara. He is known as the "father of modern karate."

In Okinawa, unarmed combat art forms initially inspired by Chinese fist-fighting were known as Ti, translating to "hand." This evolved into the term Todi, meaning "Chinese hand." By the late nineteenth century, Todi had been incorporated into the physical education programs of schools in Okinawa and was later given the name "karate," a different pronunciation (*kun'yomi*) of the *kanji* characters for Todi (唐手).

Kanō Jigorō,[15] the founder of Kodokan Judo, showed an early interest in Okinawan karate. The first time it was introduced to the mainland was at a public display by Funakoshi Gichin and

---

15 1860–1938, Japanese educator, founder of Kodokan Judo, first Asian IOC member, first president of what is now known as the Japan Sports Association. Kanō is also referred to as the "Father of Judo" and the "Father of Physical Education" in Japan.

Gima Shinkin[16] on May 17, 1922.[17] Funakoshi and Gima performed their demonstration at the Kodokan. Funakoshi began with a rendition of the Kushanku Kata, followed by Gima's Naihanchi Kata. Finally, the two of them demonstrated *kumite*, a set of paired techniques that exhibit how they are applied. After witnessing the demonstration, Kanō shared with Funakoshi his respect for Okinawan karate as a combat discipline and proposed his support in advancing the art should Funakoshi desire it.

Kanō Jigorō was a Japanese educator and the founder of judo, derived from traditional jujutsu. He played a significant role in integrating martial arts into physical education in Japanese schools. His influence in the development of modern budo and sports in Japan cannot be overstated.

At that time, Kanō was a distinguished educator in Japan and was instrumental in karate's initial establishment in Tokyo. His support was vital, and without it, karate might not have found a foothold in Japan. As interest grew, increasing demands for demonstrations and lessons prompted Funakoshi to proactively to disseminate the karate across the mainland.

Funakoshi resided in the Meiseijuku, a dormitory established for Okinawan students in Tokyo. He commandeered the lecture hall as a temporary dojo. These humble beginnings paved the way for Okinawan karate to flourish in Japan.

---

16 1896–1989, Japanese karateka.
17 Fujiwara Ryōzō, *Kakutōgi no Rekishi* (Baseball Magazine Sha, 1990) p. 656.

Later, Motobu Chōki,[18] Miyagi Chōjun,[19] Mabuni Kenwa[20] and other outstanding masters came from Okinawa to Japan one after another. Funakoshi served as the Shihan (head instructor) for clubs created at the University of Tokyo, Takushoku University, Waseda University, Hosei University, Keio University, and others. Karate spread mainly around the Kanto and Kansai regions, and students were key to its development. Later on, the *kanji* for karate = 唐手 (Chinese hand) was changed to 空手 = empty hand.[21]

Takudai Karate Exponents Launching out into the World

In 1929, Masatomo Takagi entered Takushoku University and joined Funakoshi's private karate school in the Meiseijuku. The following year in 1930, Takagi introduced karate to Takudai students, and a club was born. In 1939, the first exclusive karate dojo on the mainland, Shotokan, was built in Zōshigaya, Tokyo, by Funakoshi Gigō, the third son of Funakoshi Gichin. Funakoshi is said to be the founder of the *"Shōtōkan-ryū"* style, but the name of the school was coined after the war and Funakoshi himself never claimed his teachings to be an exclusive *ryū* (school or tradition) per se.[22]

In November 1948, the Japan Karate Association (Nihon Karate Kyōkai) was established, with Funakoshi appointed as the chief technical advisor. The core members of the association were comprised of Takudai Karate Club alumni.

Nakayama Masatoshi, as the inaugural Chief Instructor of the JKA, set about creating a structured training program to train

---

18 1870–1944, founder Motobu-ryū, and first Shihan of Toyo University's karate club.
19 1888–1953, founder of Gōjū-ryū, first Shihan of Ritsumeikan University and Doshisha University karate clubs.
20 1889–1952, founder of Shitō-ryū, first Shihan of Kansai University's karate club.
21 For a detailed analysis of the early days of karate in Japan and how it evolved, refer to *Karate Its History and Practice* (Nippon Budokan, 2021) by Koyama Masashi, Wada Kōji, Kadekaru Tōru, and translated by Alexander Bennett
22 Funakoshi's pen name, "Shōtō" (松涛), means "waving pines." This is where the name Shōtōkan comes from.

teachers. In 1956, Kanazawa Hirokazu became one of the first train-
ees to pass the program, and was destined to teach karate in over
120 countries worldwide. The culture and philosophy of Takudai
was perfectly aligned with the JKA's mission to dispatch specialist
instructors globally. Graduates of the Takudai Karate Club traveled
far and wide and dedicated themselves to spreading the practice of
karate. Thus, OSU/OSS also spread beyond Japan's shores.

JKA Honbu Shihan, Shiina Katsutoshi.

Past Overseas Karate Instructors from Takudai Karate Club

America	• Nishiyama Hidetaka • Okazaki Teruyuki • Mori Masataka • Kisaka Katsuji
Mexico	• Yagashira Nobuhiro • Tabata Yūkichi
Brazil	• Higashino Tetsuma • Uryu Sadamu • Sagara Juichi • Tanaka Yasutaka • Takeuchi Tadashi
Great Britain	• Enoeda Keinosuke • Asano Shirō • Kawazoe Masao • Ōta Yoshinobu
Italy	• Miura Masaru • Takahashi Katsutarō
Australia	• Kawasoe Norio
Germany	• Ochi Hideo • Nagai Akio • Tsuchiya Shuichi • Akita Shinji
Spain	• Aoki Osamu
Belgium	• Miyazaki Tetsu
Greece	• Kawada Minoru
Thailand	• Ōmura Fujikiyo
Taiwan	• Asai Tetsuhiko • Ushijima Hiroshi • Yamada Yōsuke
Malaysia	• Habu Yoshiki • Hayashi Ken'ichi

This list is by no means exhaustive. Shiina Katsutoshi, Naka Tatsuya, Taniyama Takuya, Murakami Manabu, and many others currently travel to various parts of the world to teach karate.

JKA Honbu Shihan, Taniyama Takuya. *SKIF Shuseki Shihan, Murakami Manabu.*

JKA Honbu Shihan, Naka Tatsuya

Column 2: Karate Instructor Decorated by the German Government for "OSS"

Nagai Akio upon receiving the Cross of Merit from the German government in 2002.

Nagai Akio was a Takudai graduate who went to Germany in 1965 to instruct karate. He is an instructor for SKIF, which is why OSS is used here instead of OSU. In May 2002, he was awarded the prestigious "Bundesverdienstkreuz am Bande" (Cross of Merit) by the Federal Republic of Germany for his many years of contribution to society through his teaching. In accepting the award, Nagai stated,

"The Takudai spirit of OSS enabled me to teach and connect with my students in a country where I did not understand the language well for 36 years. Through OSS, we shared our joys, sorrows, and hardships. We used OSS frequently, so much so that we became known as the 'OSS Ensemble' to the staff at the Japanese Consulate in Dusseldorf. In my opinion, receiving this medal was due to the Takudai OSS spirit."

When Nagai received the award in 2002, it was revealed that the former German Chancellor had taken received karate lessons from him while he was a student. It makes one wonder if the Chancellor didn't also use OSS as a means of communication.

Five Great Takudai Martial Artists

1. Nakayama Masatoshi – Founder of the Modern Karate Movement

In 1932, when Nakayama Masatoshi entered Takushoku University, he harbored a deep aspiration to explore the world and leave a lasting impact. It was during his time at Takudai that he discovered karate, a discipline that would shape the rest of his professional and personal journey. Graduating in 1937 with ambitions of studying overseas, he journeyed to China as an exchange student. He subsequently spent nearly a decade working for a government agency there before making his way back to Japan. Upon his return, Nakayama began giving karate lessons at Takudai, ultimately securing a position as a physical education instructor at the university by 1954.

Beyond teaching karate to students, Nakayama was instrumental in introducing the martial art to Allied military bases. This initiative began around 1948 when military personnel stationed in

Nakayama Masatoshi, a highly respected karate master from Japan (1913-87). He was instrumental in establishing the Japan Karate Association (JKA) in 1949 and wrote numerous influential textbooks on karate, significantly contributing to its global popularity. For nearly 40 years, until his death, Nakayama dedicated himself to the international dissemination of Shotokan karate. He was the first in Shotokan history to receive the 9th Dan rank during his lifetime, and he was awarded the 10th Dan posthumously.

Japan, particularly those at U.S. Air Force bases, expressed interest in learning karate and other budo. In response, Nakayama and other budo experts organized introductory demonstrations and seminars at various locations. These experts included Nakayama Hakudō for kendo, Mifune Kyūzō for judo, Tomiki Kenji for aikido, and others. For karate, both alumni and active members of university clubs participated.

Nakayama, along with members of the Takudai Karate Club, made regular visits to military bases, conducting sessions twice a week at different locations. This routine, which spanned approximately four years, involved traveling from one base to another, leading to their being affectionately dubbed the "Nakayama Circus" due to their extensive and dynamic outreach efforts.

Lieutenant Emilio "Mel" Bruno,[1] a physical education instructor in the USAF, became fascinated with karate around 1952 and made it his mission to spread it in the military. He organized a training program for a delegation of approximately 12 physical education officials from the US Strategic Air Force. They traveled to Japan to undergo three months of intensive karate instruction under Nakayama's guidance.

After completing their training, these officials returned to the United States or other USAF bases worldwide, where they disseminated the karate by incorporating it into physical education programs. This initiative was repeated four times, highlighting the strong commitment of the US military to integrating karate into their training regimen.

In 1953, the USAF escalated its commitment to martial arts by inviting a Japanese delegation headed by judo expert Kotani Sumiyuki for a three-month instructional tour across several air bases in the United States. Accompanying this tour were Nishiyama Hidetaka, an alumnus of Takudai, and two other karate specialists. This facilitated the spread of both judo and karate, showcasing the depth and versatility of budo to American military personnel.

The karate style that Funakoshi Gichin brought from Okinawa to the Japanese mainland in the 1920s was primarily focused on *kata*, or form training, which involves systematic patterns of movements. During that period, budo disciplines such as kendo, with its matches using protective gear, and judo, with its *randori* (sparring sessions), were becoming more competitive and popular. Naturally, karate practitioners started to seek ways to apply their skills in a more dynamic setting, beyond the predetermined movements of *kata*, and test themselves in actual sparring scenarios.

Funakoshi, however, was not keen on the introduction of competitive *kumite*. He feared that if he permitted students to engage

---

1 1914–2003. American judo practitioner (6th Dan).

freely in *kumite*, they would become obsessed with matches and forget the fundamentals of *kata*. Despite his misgivings, Funakoshi was unable to curb student enthusiasm for the thrill of competition.

As karate evolved to include more competitive elements, prioritizing the safety of practitioners became a major concern. To address this, the concept of the *sundome* rule was introduced, where a fighter stops an attack just before making full contact with the opponent's body. This approach to "controlled combat" was developed incrementally through trial and error, and was eventually adopted into various karate schools.

This methodology laid the groundwork for the rules used in the karate competition at the 2020 Tokyo Olympics, as established by the World Karate Federation (WKF). Nakayama Masatoshi played a pivotal role in the development and formalization of these safety-oriented competitive rules, marking a substantial contribution to modern karate's regulatory framework.

Nakayama, however, did not like using the term *sundome*. He believed that it contradicted the concept of *ichigeki-hissatsu*, or one-hit kill, which emphasizes the need for maximum force in a strike. To him, it was like stepping on the gas and brake pedals of a car simultaneously. He described it in different terms. In karate, Nakayama taught, the aim is not to stop the strike before impact, but rather to aim the strike just before the opponent's vital point and deliver a devastating blow with "*kime*" there instead. Therefore, the strike doesn't hit the opponent's body directly because that is not the real target.

Nakayama placed emphasis on *kime*, or focus of the blow, as a fundamental aspect of karate. He believed that without *kime*, the integral link between *kata* and *kumite* is lost, reducing *kumite* to merely a competition to identify winners and losers rather than an expression of martial skill and discipline. Furthermore, without *kime*, *zanshin* — the critical state of vigilant awareness and readiness for further action after executing a technique, which is essential in all budo — would also diminish. *Zanshin* embodies the principle that one must always remain alert and prepared for a counterattack from any direction, even after a successful strike. The JKA regards *zanshin* as a core element, viewing it as central to understanding karate not just as a sport but as a true budo.

The 1st National Karate Championship Tournament was held In October 1957. The winner of the *kumite* division was Kanazawa Hirokazu. From this point on, karate on the mainland developed into a competitive sport, and within a short period of time it spread throughout the world. Although in many ways this trend was contrary to Funakoshi's philosophy, Nakayama's efforts to promote karate as a competitive sport has led him to be referred to as the "founder of modern karate."

2. Mas Ōyama – Founder of Kyokushin Karate

Ōyama Masutatsu,[2] commonly known as Mas Ōyama in the Western world, revolutionized karate by introducing the knockdown rule. This rule allowed competitors to use their bare hands and feet to inflict as much damage as possible on their opponent without the use of protective gear. However, direct attacks to the face with the hands were not permitted. The winner of the match was determined by who successfully knocked down their opponent using valid techniques. In September 1969, the 1st Open Tournament All-Japan Karate Championship, the earliest competition to adopt the knockdown rule system, was won by Yamazaki Terutomo.

Using an effective mass media strategy, Ōyama's Kyokushin Kaikan gained a massive following from the 1970s to the 1990s.

In 1939, Ōyama moved to Japan from Korea and began studying Shotokan karate under Funakoshi Gichin and Gōjū-ryū karate with Yamaguchi Gōgen. During the war, Ōyama was enrolled at Takushoku University, but he was never a member of the karate club.

---

2 1923–1994. Karate practitioner originally from Korea, and founder of Kyokushin Kaikan karate.

Ōyama Masutatsu, also widely known as Mas Oyama, was born Choi Yeong-eui on July 27, 1923, in South Korea. An ethnic Korean, he moved to Japan where he spent most of his life and became a Japanese citizen in 1968. Ōyama was a renowned karate master who established Kyokushin Kaikan Karate, the pioneering and impactful style of full contact karate. He passed away on April 26, 1994, leading to fragmentation of his Kyokushin empire.

According to numerous alumni of the club, Nakayama Masatoshi informed them that Ōyama stayed at Takudai only until his sophomore year. So why did he choose Takushoku University? Ōyama explained the reasons for his decision:

> "When I decided to attend Takudai, one of the main reasons was because I knew Kimura Masahiko was studying there. To me, Kimura was the embodiment of a true warrior and my personal modern-day Miyamoto Musashi. I was in awe of him and held him in the highest regard."[3]

Ōyama Masutatsu made his way to the United States in March of 1952 to promote karate. This marked the beginning of Kyokushin's

---

3 Motoi Saesato, *Ōyama Masutatsu no Shinjitsu* (Kitensha, 1997), pp.77–78.

Gōgen Yamaguchi (1909 – 1989), a disciple of Chōjun Miyagi in Gōjū-ryū Karate, established the International Karate-dō Gōjū Kai Association. Widely recognized in the karate community as "the Cat" due to his small stature, standing just over five feet tall and weighing 160 pounds, Yamaguchi was noted for his commanding presence that seemed much larger. His nickname, "the Cat," originated from American GIs who observed his smooth walk and flowing hair. Yamaguchi played a pivotal role in popularizing Gōjū-ryū globally, leading to hundreds of thousands of people practicing this style in both traditional and modern karate schools around the world.

worldwide expansion. By June of 1956, he had founded the Ōyama Dojo in Ikebukuro, Tokyo. It was eventually restructured as Kyokushin Kaikan in May of 1964.

Nakamura Tadashi,[4] one of Ōyama's junior colleagues, moved to New York in 1966 to teach Kyokushin. He also took his teachings to South America, Europe, and New Zealand. Ōyama Shigeru[5] also began teaching in 1967, starting in Connecticut and later expanding throughout the United States, South America, Europe, New Zealand, and Jamaica. Kyokushin Karate eventually gained popularity in Europe during the 1970s, with the likes of Dutchmen Loek Hollander and Jon Bluming introducing it to the continent.

---

4 1942–. World Seido Karate Organization president.

5 Ōyama Shigeru (1936-2016) became a prominent figure in the world of karate. For over 50 years, he ran a dojo in New York, where he taught Kyokushin karate to numerous students. In 1985, he established his own organization, known as World Oyama Karate. Oyama is recognized as one of the first Kyokushin practitioners to successfully finish the 100-man *kumite*. He is not related by blood to Mas Oyama.

Takudai's OSU tradition was adopted into Kyokushin Karate by Ōyama probably because of the time he spent at the university. The world's karate population is said to be 50-million, or even 100-million according to some estimates. Although it is impossible to get an exact figure the number of karate schools in existence, arguably the most widespread are related to Shotokan (founded by Funakoshi Gichin), and Kyokushin. As these two major schools spread domestically and internationally, OSU became a truly ubiquitous term.

Kyokushin Kaikan's OSU

Mas Ōyama once said, "My karate can be found everywhere. Whatever the country, the language used in the dojo is Japanese. Everything starts and ends with OSU."[6] He also said the following about his understanding of the deeper meaning of OSU.

> "OSU is not just about putting up with hardships, it's also about being a decent human being while being strict with oneself. But there are some who get it all wrong and use their booming voices to scare others, which is a mistake. These folks end up bowing only to those who are stronger than them, and that's just sad. The real deal with OSU is to have a sympathetic heart for the weak, and the drive to take on mighty opponents without giving up. Plus, there's the aspect of supporting and motivating each other to exceed all boundaries and reach the top."[7]

From the *fudō-dachi* stance (feet shoulder-width apart, hands clasped and placed in front of the hips), both arms are crossed in

---

6 *Asahi Journal* (22 July 1983), p. 4
7 *GORO*, (Shōgakkan, 12 August 1976), p. 41

front of the chest and OSU is shouted with a large swing down of the arms. This is now the greeting used in Kyokushin. However, in the early days of the All-Japan Kyokushin Championships, the pre-match standing bow was performed with the fingertips straightened in the *ki wo tsuke* (attention) posture. When did this change to the current form?

Testimony - Yamazaki Terutomo

"During my competitive years there was no such thing the crossed-handed bow like we see today. We just bowed from the stand-at-attention position. I was never taught to do it any other way by Ōya-ma-sensei. I think that the '*fudō-dachi*' bow evolved over time to include the exaggerated hand gestures that we see today. *Kata* performances are now started this way as well..."

If you check the videos of past Kyokushin All-Japan Championships and World Championships, you will notice that a normal mutual standing bow was performed from the *ki-wo-tsuke* posture. This changed to bowing from the *fudō-dachi* stance (arms uncrossed), and eventually to bowing with hands crossed in front of the chest. However, looking at recent Kyokushin standing bows, there are those who cross their hands but do not actually perform a bow. In other words, crossing hands in front of the body has become synonymous with bowing.

"OSU no Futamoji" (The Two Kanji for OSU)

Yamazaki Terutomo, who was known as the "Dragon of Kyokushin," and Soeno Yoshiji,[8] the so-called "Tiger of Kyokushin," loved to sing the song *"OSU no Futamoji"* when they were students.

1

Gritting my teeth through the torturous training,
I've pushed myself to make it this far.
With the three letters of OSU[9] etched deep in my heart,
I keep on going, chasing my star.

2

The black belt is my ultimate goal,
A lifelong dream that I'll achieve.
Pouring my soul into those three letters OSU,
I'll risk it all, to prove what I believe.

3

As I close my eyes, tears fall like rain,
Muffled sobs of regret and pain.
OSU echoes in my troubled heart,
Sleep won't come, as I drown in disdain.

4

I stake my body on every strike,
No room for doubts or sinister ploy.
With OSU burning like fire in my soul,
Karate is my life, my ultimate joy.

Mas Ōyama once answered the question "What is OSU?" in the readers' Q&A section of the Kyokushin in-house magazine "Power Karate" (August 1981 edition). He responded, "Like the song, it means to bite down with your back teeth and endure. This is the true spirit of *bu* (martial arts), and the philosophy of Kyokushin."

---

8 1947–. Japanese karate practitioner. Currently the director of the World Karate Association Shidokan and runner up in the 1st Kyokushin All-Japan Full Contact Karate Championships.
9 The original Japanese says "two characters for OSU," but the translator adapted this phrase to three letters in line with how the word is spelled in English.

Ishikawa Tadashi, an alumnus of Takudai Karate Club, contributed the following article to the commemorative publication *Fifty-Year History of Takudai Karate Club.*

"I never won anything in 1967. I composed this poem in my diary the night I was eliminated in the semi-final round. I had reached an impasse in my technique and was mentally exhausted.

Tears of regret when I close my eyes,
I hush my voice sobbing in lament.
The three letters OSU make my heart ache,
And, slumber is denied through this discontent."[10]

This, of course, is a rendition of the third verse of from "*OSU no Futamoji.*"

Testimony - Soeno Yoshiji

"I learned this song from Sakurai Ryōji, a senior of the Takudai Kendo Club who lived in my neighborhood. I taught it to everyone else."

The song seems to have been forgotten by members of the Takudai Karate Club now, but it is still sung at the Nihon University Kickboxing Club founded by Yamazaki Terutomo while he was a student there. It is also sung by members of the Jōsai University Karate Club, founded by Soeno Yoshiji. Soeno's junior at Jōsai, Takagi Kaoru, became head of the Hokkaido branch of the Kyokushin Kaikan, and his students have continued to belt out the song for generations.

---

10 Takushoku University Karate Club Alumni Association, *Takushoku University Reisawa-kai Karate Club 50-nen Shi* (1979), p.72

According to Takagi Kaoru's student, Hirotomi Tsukasa, "I learned the song from Master Takagi when I became a black belt, and I often rattle it off at parties." This demonstrates another route through which traditions spread from Takudai to Kyokushin.

Mas Ōyama and Iijima Isamu

During the turbulent postwar era, a showdown took place between two men: Mas Ōyama, a Korean national, and a Japanese named Iijima Isamu.

First, who was Iijima Isamu? He was a judoka who graduated from Takudai. After fighting in Mongolia he was later dispatched to Beijing. While there, he connected with Mikami Takashi,[11] who was involved in the 1932 May 15 Incident, a plot to assassinate Prime Minister Tōjō Hideki.[12] Mikami was in Beijing to procure weapons and funds for the mission. In addition, Iijima crossed paths in Tianjin with Masatomo Takagi, founder of Takudai's karate club, and Nakayama Masatoshi.

Following his commissioning as a second lieutenant in the army, Iijima requested to be stationed once again in Mongolia, yet destiny intervened. He was diagnosed with pulmonary tuberculosis, a disease considered incurable then, and was forced into to prolonged hospitalization, during which he observed Japan's capitulation. Initially, Iijima contemplated death as his only escape but ultimately rejected the notion of suicide. His determination was unwavering - he resolved that even in the face of his nation's downfall, he himself would not succumb.

What follows is a detailed account of the intense confrontation between Ōyama and Iijima, as narrated by nonfiction writer Futoshi Kitanokuchi. Drawing on first-hand accounts from Iijima's students, Kitanokuchi paints a vivid picture of the tense standoff between the

---

11 1905–1971. Lieutenant of the Imperial Navy and a prominent nationalist.
12 1884–1948. Imperial Army soldier, politician, and 40th Prime Minister of Japan.

two warriors.

"During the post-war era, Iijima struggled with health issues and spent his time wandering the Shinjuku Station West Exit black market, today known as Yamiichi, and the adjoining pathways to the East Exit. In this bustling environment, he witnessed a shocking scene: an American soldier openly attacking a Japanese woman in the middle of the day. Despite the gravity of the situation, the *yakuza* and other Japanese men who managed the black market ignored the egregious assault. Enraged by the inaction and the assault, Iijima leapt into action, using his expert *uchimata* judo technique to take down two soldiers. However, his intervention led to a tense confrontation with the Military Police who soon arrived at the scene. The situation quickly intensified, and Iijima was apprehended at gunpoint, then swiftly taken to the US Eighth Army Stockade in Nakano. This event was the first instance of a Japanese person attacking an American soldier since the conclusion of the war.

The black market in Tokyo was expanding rapidly due to economic limitations, and it had become a brutal battleground where various groups vied for control. Korean and Chinese gangs, Japanese *yakuza*, and even ex-soldiers were all in constant conflict. The competition was fierce, and it was nearly impossible to navigate the treacherous waters of this underground world unscathed. The black market was an unimaginable cesspool of cutthroat rivalry.

Iijima, who had reached a level of notoriety for attacking an American soldier post-defeat, was admired by the black market's leaders for his charismatic presence. Mikami Taku, a stakeholder in the market, once approached Iijima for help with a group of Koreans residing unlawfully in a dormitory. Many Koreans had been forced to work in Japanese mines and factories during the war and were left to fend for themselves upon their release. In these difficult times, both Japanese and Koreans suffered. With the police force largely ineffective, Iijima assumed the responsibility of safeguarding properties owned by Japanese citizens.

Iijima was greeted in the dormitory supervisor's office by Mas Ōyama. Ōyama had just been discharged as a mechanic in the Imperial Naval Air Force and was working hard to liberate his countrymen as a member of the League of Koreans, an organization established in Japan after the war. Incidentally, Ōyama's name before his naturalization in Japan was Choi Young Eui, and his post-naturalization Japanese name, "Masutatsu" (倍達), is a patriotic term in Korean similar in sentiment to the Japanese word "Yamato" (大和).

In a tense confrontation, Ōyama approached Iijima and slammed his fists down on the table with a menacing look in his eyes. He was furious and ready to fight. 'You dirty bastard!' he shouted. 'If you want to kick us out, you'd better come armed with a pistol or a dagger because I'll make short shrift of you!' Iijima sat quietly, facing off against the fiery Ōyama. It was a clash between a Japanese nationalist and a Korean nationalist, each determined to come out on top.

After Ōyama's angry outburst subsided, Iijima spoke with a calm intensity in his voice. 'I'll take you on,' he said. Ōyama straightened up, intrigued by Iijima's boldness. Despite recovering from pulmonary tuberculosis, Iijima sat there with an unyielding look that never wavered. Ōyama was taken aback and asked, 'Who the hell are you anyway?' Iijima answered simply and with conviction, 'I'm Iijima from Takudai.'

Ōyama enrolled at Takudai because of his admiration for the peerless judoka Kimura Masahiko. Ōyama was also a member of the East Asia League Association founded by Ishiwara Kanji, so in addition to the Takudai connection, the two of them actually had a lot in common politically speaking. After the dormitory incident, Ōyama visited Iijima at his home, bringing him butter, which was a precious commodity at the time. Ōyama said to Iijima, 'You're too thin. Eat this butter and fatten yourself up…'

… In those days, Iijima was making a living as a 'dojo-breaker.' Teaming up with Shioda Gōzō (founder of Yōshinkan aikido) and OBs from Takudai's judo and karate clubs, the group would visit judo and police dojos in Tokyo and challenge its members to matches. After obliterating their hapless foe, they would extort some kind of payment in exchange for the dojo sign which they would claim as a trophy."[13]

Shioda briefly touches on these days in his book.

---

13 Kitanokuchi Futoshi, *Shakunetsu Reppaku no Shisui* (Tenzandōjin, 2009), pp. 20–22

"Mr. Iijima managed to get his hands on a Jeep and would drive us to the police dojos every day. I have many interesting stories to tell about this time... I'll leave it at that..."[14]

Perhaps he thought those interesting stories from back in the day were best left unsaid.

Ogura Shōichirō was another man closely associated with both Iijima and Ōyama. Ogura founded a right-wing student organization when he entered Takushoku University. He started attending Ōyama's dojo the following year, and later served as an instructor for the Brazilian branch of the Kyokushin Kaikan.

Testimony – Ogura Shōichirō

"I worked with Mr. Iijima from 1968 to 1972 (Ogura was the head of the "Action Team" of Tokubetsu Bōei Hoshō Corporation, a security company established by Iijima). I learned firsthand about the encounter between him and Ōyama-sensei. He recounted Ōyama-sensei's intense display, hammering away at the table. Iijima, however, maintained the demeanor of a gentleman. He possessed a commanding presence, enveloping everyone in his vicinity with his aura. He simply exuded an undeniable gravitas."

Ogura currently serves as an advisor for Ashihara Kaikan. He was with the founder, Ashihara Hideyuki,[15] right to the end. Ashihara composed a song titled "*Hōrōka.*" It is based on "*Moko Hōrōka,*" a favorite Takudai song about wandering through the plains of

---

14 Shioda Gōzō, *Shioda Gōzō no Aikidō Jinsei* (Kaimeisha, 2012) p. 169
15 1944–1995. Japanese karateka, former Kyokushinkai Ehime Branch Chief, and founder of Ashihara Kaikan.

Mongolia. Although never a student there himself, Ashihara was drawn to the raw and gritty vibe of Takudai and would often visit Ogura there just to soak up the atmosphere and hang out.

A rare photograph of Ashihara Hideyuki on the left receiving a kick from Ogura Shōichirō, with Mas Ōyama watching on from the seat in the middle.

3. Shioda Gōzō – Yōshinkan Aikido Founder

Despite his small frame, standing at 154 cm tall and weighing only 47 kg, Shioda Gōzō, the founder of Yōshinkan, was esteemed as a martial arts virtuoso. In May 1932, at the young age of 16 and already holding a 3rd Dan black belt in judo, Shioda visited Ueshiba Morihei, the founder of aikido. Ueshiba confidently challenged Shioda to attack him in any manner. When Shioda surprisingly attempted a kick, Ueshiba swiftly and effortlessly threw him onto his back, leaving Shioda astounded and puzzled by the swift counter. Awed by Ueshiba's prowess, Shioda immediately requested to become his disciple.

In 1933, Shioda began his pre-college studies at Takudai, where he met the judoka Kimura Masahiko, who was two years his junior. Shioda took a leave of absence from the university for two years to train as an *uchideshi* under the guidance of Ueshiba. Upon returning to Takudai, Shioda found himself in the same class as Kimura.

After completing their studies in 1941, Shioda was assigned to administrative roles in China, Taiwan, and Borneo. He returned to Japan in 1946 and resumed intensive aikido training with Ueshiba. In 1955, he created the Yoshinkan style of aikido, known for its focus on self-defense techniques. The name "Yoshinkan" came from the name of the judo dojo operated by Shioda's father. Two years later, Shioda initiated a significant partnership with the Tokyo Metropolitan Police Department. The following words were written by Shioda:

"I had the greatest experiences of my life at Takudai. I dressed in traditional attire and always carried books around with me. My reading material usually consisted of works on philosophy, patriotism, continental or international affairs. One book that was particularly encouraged among Takudai students was Ōkawa Shūmei's *A Study of the Japanese Spirit* (1924). We

Shioda Gōzō (1915 – 1994) was a renowned Japanese aikido master and the founder of the Yōshinkan school of aikido. He was among the most distinguished students of Ueshiba Morihei, the originator of aikido.

would often gather in a circle on the lawn and engage in discussions about the current state of our nation.

Takudai students always impressed me with their boldness. Their kimonos were torn, caps tattered, and they had towels hanging from their waists and wooden clogs on their feet. The upperclassmen were domineering, and their juniors were submissive. Despite the strict etiquette, Takudai had a comfortable atmosphere that enveloped the university with an indescribable sense of harmony. The upperclassmen loved the juniors, and the juniors adored them back. *Senpai* would readily take the fall for juniors and generously lend them their wallets when they were broke. The Takudai traditions were cherished by all.

Despite defeat, Takudai managed to survive and continue its mission and function. However, it cannot be denied that the university has lost its grandiose dreams of the past and has become smaller in scale, and more petty-bourgeois in nature. Interestingly, it seems that foreigners are now more interested in Japanese budo than the Japanese themselves. What is happening? It's time for the Japanese to wake up from their slumber!" [16]

In other book, Shioda states, "My friend Kimura Masahiko once said, 'As modern judo doesn't employ strikes (*atemi*), it has much to learn from aikido from the standpoint of self-defense.' Kimura was a real warrior who had seen a lot. He knew about the importance

16 *Tsuitō Shioda Gōzō* (November 1995) pp. 3–6

of *atemi* in real combat."[17] He also talks of his friendship with Nakayama Masatoshi.

> "Before Nakayama Masatoshi of Shotokan passed away, I shared a strong bond with him. Mr. Nakayama approached me with a request to instruct his trainees in the bodywork techniques of aikido. I spent approximately one month teaching at Shotokan. Among those who attended was Kanazawa Hirokazu, who has since become an independent karate instructor. Even at that time he was known as a karate force, and his proficiency in aikido was unmatched by any of his peers."[18]

Kanazawa Hirokazu also shared his personal experiences with Shioda in the following account:

> "During my time at Takudai, I looked up to three of my *senpai* who had already made a name for themselves in budo. Kimura Masahiko, Shioda Gōzō, and Nakayama Masatoshi were their names. Their reputation preceded them, and they seemed to exist on a different plane than us regular students, as if walking on clouds."[19]

On March 29, 2016, I had an opportunity to speak with Inoue Kyōichi, the second Kanchō of Yōshinkan.

> "I entered the newly-founded Yōshinkan in the Shinjuku ward of Tokyo in 1955. Shioda-sensei was

---

17 Shioda Gōzō, *Aikidō Shugyō* (Takeuchi Shoten Shinsha, 1991), p.156
18 Ibid., pp. 157–158.
19 *Tsuitō Shioda Gōzō* (November 1995), pp. 79–80.

a graduate of Takudai and used OSU a lot. Natu-
rally, we started to use it as well. Shioda-sensei said,
'At Takudai, we just don't say yes. It's always OSU.
No matter what your *senpai* say to you, respond with
OSU.' He told me to never hesitate with this reply.
It was around 1960 when students at the aikido club
at Takudai came to practice at the Yōshinkan Honbu
Dojo. The Takudai members only said OSU.

Me: 'Do you understand?'
Takudai student: 'OSU!'
Me: 'Do you not understand?'
Takudai student: 'OSU!'
Me: 'Which is it?!'
Takudai student: 'OSU!'
Me: 'What do you mean by OSU?!'
Takudai student: 'OSU!'

That's what our daily conversations were like. I still
use OSU with my aikido friends and other martial
artists. In 1970, I was sent to the Metropolitan Police
Department to teach aikido to police officers. I was
informed by one of the superiors there that saying
OSU all the time was probably not a good idea.

At Yōshinkan, OSU became a common greeting,
especially when addressing Shioda-sensei. However,
the usage of OSU has decreased since his passing.
When I travel to teach aikido abroad, I've noticed
that more practitioners use OSU in their dojos than
in Japan. They don't simply walk past each other; they
stop, bow, and quietly say OSU as a sign of respect. It's
heartening to see that the true spirit of budo has been

Kimura Masahiko (1917–93) was a renowned Japanese judoka and professional wrestler, often regarded as the finest judoka ever. He made history by winning the All-Japan Judo Championships three consecutive times, a first in the sport, and he remained undefeated in judo competitions from 1936 to 1950. He is pictured here after winning the Emperor's Tenran Tournament in 1940.

effectively transmitted to them. When I meet these foreign practitioners, I'm grateful for their understanding and appreciation of our art."

4. The Strongest Judoka – Kimura Masahiko

The saying "There was no Kimura before Kimura, and there will be no Kimura after Kimura" speaks to Kimura Masahiko's unrivaled greatness in the world of judo. It is believed to have originated from Tomita Tsuneo, the author of the famous novel Sugata Sanshirō.

Kimura's judo skills were unparalleled, earning him the distinction of being considered the greatest judoka of all time. He was awarded a 4th Dan in judo by the Kodokan during his final year of junior high school. In 1935, he enrolled in Takudai's prep school, where he won the prestigious Meiji Jingū Shrine Tournament. In his third year at the prep school, he won the All-Japan Judo Championships in 1937. In 1940, Kimura's fame skyrocketed after he won all five of his matches decisively by *ippon* in the Tenran Budo Tournament, an event held to celebrate Japan's 2600th anniversary.

Until his retirement in 1950, Kimura won the All-Japan Judo Championships for 13 consecutive years, an unprecedented record. After graduating from Takudai in 1941, Kimura worked as a professional judoka, and then transitioned to professional wrestling making his debut in 1954 after a tour of Brazil. His one-on-one bout with Rikidōzan in October of the same year caused quite a stir, but more on that soon.

Kimura and Shioda reminisced about their Takudai days in a 1987 magazine interview.

> Kimura: "Shioda and I once had an arm-wrestling match. Man, he was strong. I was 170cm, 85kg, and
>
> Shioda was 154cm, 47kg."
>
> Shioda: "Kimura told somebody that he arm-wrestled me 10 times and lost each match. The truth is that we only did it three times. I won the first two and took it easy on the third one (laughs)."
>
> Kimura: "When I was in college, I was a live-in student at Ushijima Tatsukuma-sensei's place. I'd get up at 4:30 in the morning and clean the house. After that, I would do *makiwara* training, punching the straw board a thousand times with each hand. The *makiwara* strengthened my thumbs, arms, elbows, and wrists. Then I would go to the Metropolitan

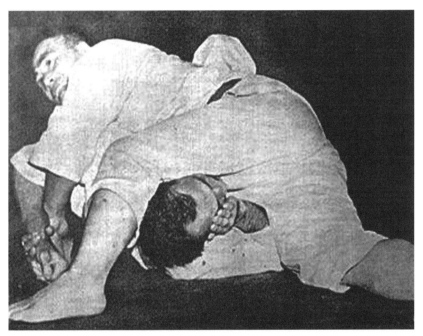

An iconic moment in martial arts history: Kimura Masahiko employs the devastating ude-garami technique against Hélio Gracie during their legendary 1951 bout.

Police Department dojo and practice for over an hour from around 10:00 a.m. After this I trained at the Takudai dojo for three hours, at the Kodokan from 6:00 p.m., and then at the Fukagawa dojo from 8:00 p.m.

I would go back to the Ushijima residence to eat. I'd take a bath and start practicing on my own. Solo training would consist of 1,000 push-ups and then weights. I'd bench press 600 reps of 80 kg.

Then, I would tie a judo belt around the maple tree and practice *uchikomi*. The belts would wear through in no time after a thousand times a day. It cost me a lot of money, so I switched to ropes. After that, I practiced *ōsoto-gari* throws. The important thing with *ōsoto-gari* is to 'reap' with the leg. I would stand on one leg holding a thin branch in my hand and do the reaping movement a thousand times. I would put about 30 candles behind me and try to blow the candles out with the wind generated by my leg reaping. At first, only about three candles would go out, but after three months, I managed to extinguish them all. I moved the candles further apart to make the task more difficult.

By the time I completed that task, it would be 2:00 a.m., yet I would not go to sleep. To me, sleeping felt akin to dying. I was determined to stay alive to continue my practice. I believed that with such training, I would never lose my edge. To stay awake, I would pinch myself all over. I conditioned myself to forego sleep, often staying awake until 4:00 a.m., when I began to clean the house. The secret to handling this was simple: I slept during my college classes."

Shioda: "Yeah, you were always sleeping in class!"[20]

Kimura Masahiko vs. Hélio Gracie

The Ultimate Fighting Championship (UFC) is an organization that currently reigns supreme in martial arts entertainment. Its first event, UFC 1, took place in Denver, Colorado in November 1993 and was produced by Rorion Gracie, a member of the renowned Gracie family, who are credited with developing Brazilian Jiu-jitsu.

The competition was held in a wire mesh cage called the "Octagon" where there is no escape. The only prohibited actions are biting and eye gouging. A diverse group of fighters, including boxers, karate practitioners, kick boxers, wrestlers, and others participated in the tournament. The winner was Royce Gracie, Rorion's younger brother.

At the time, the Gracie style was relatively unknown, but the family's plan to promote it through this event was a roaring success. Royce won UFC 2 the following year, and his brother, Rickson Gracie, added to the family's reputation by defeating prominent Japanese wrestlers Takada Nobuhiko[21] and Funaki Masakatsu[22] in succession.

More than 40 years earlier, in July 1951, Kimura Masahiko was visiting São Paulo to teach judo with his pro wrestling tour when a silent assassin appeared. It was Hélio Gracie (father of Rorion, Rickson, and Royce). Hélio Gracie, along with his brother Carlos,

---

20 Monthly *FULL CONTACT KARATE* (Fukushōdō, December 1987) pp. 20–22
21 1962–. Japanese pro wrestler and mixed martial artist. Fought Rickson Gracie in October 1997 and October 1998, but lost both times.
22 1969–. Japanese pro wrestler and mixed martial artist. Was defeated by Rickson Gracie in May 2000 at the Tokyo Dome.

learned *jūjutsu* from Maeda Mitsuyo[23] and they later developed their own improved technical system of Gracie Jiu-jitsu, which he performed to immense effect in no-holds-barred Vale Tudo matches (bare-knuckle fighting with minimal restrictions).

Earlier that year, Kimura had transitioned into professional wrestling in Hawaii, drawn by the financial advantages of scripted bouts. He was driven by the urgent need to secure funds for costly antibiotics, specifically streptomycin, to treat his wife who was suffering from tuberculosis and had been hospitalized.

The match between Hélio and Kimura was, of course, a real fight. The idea was to brawl it out until one or the other gave up. The fight took place at the Maracana Stadium, a soccer arena constructed for the FIFA World Cup Brazil held the previous year in 1950. During World War II, Brazil and Japan were on opposing sides, fueling the Brazilian public's anticipation for this match-up. On October 23, in the presence of numerous VIPs including the Brazilian Vice President, Kimura faced Hélio. He incapacitated Hélio with an *ude-garami* armlock, breaking his arm. Despite his injury, Hélio refused to surrender. Ultimately, Kimura claimed victory by technical knockout after Hélio's corner threw in the towel to end the fight.

The birth of the term "Kimura Lock" or simply "Kimura" for the armlock in Brazilian Jiu-jitsu and mixed martial arts dates back to this match. It is believed that Hélio gave it this name as a tribute to Kimura's formidable strength. The Gracie family has long held Kimura Masahiko in the highest esteem, as he was the fighter they respected above all others. OSU (BJJ usually writes is at OSS) is a term frequently used by BJJ practitioners, although many who use it daily are unaware of its origin in Kimura's alma mater, Takudai.

---

23 1878–1941. Went to the US in 1904 to teach judo. While traveling overseas he engaged in matches with wrestlers and boxers. Also known as Conde Koma.

Kimura Masahiko vs. Rikidōzan

On December 22, 1954, Kuramae Kokugikan Sumo Arena was the venue for the highly anticipated wrestling match between Kimura and sumo great, Rikidōzan. The match attracted such a massive crowd that it surpassed the arena's capacity, drawing over 15,000 fans. Its significance was underscored by the fact that both of Japan's only two television stations at the time aired it live, reputedly achieving an unbelievable 100% viewership rating. Although few households owned a television back then, people across the country congregated around public television sets on the streets to witness this epic showdown.

Would the winner be Kimura, unbeaten in 15 years of judo? Or, would it be former sumo Sekiwake Rikidōzan?[24] The major Japanese newspapers, including *Asahi*, *Mainichi*, and *Yomiuri*, all reported on the bout of the century. Mas Ōyama was also present in Kimura's camp.

During that era, the scripted nature of professional wrestling was not widely recognized, and spectators believed they were witnessing a genuine contest. Behind the scenes, just before the match commenced, both parties agreed to a draw. *The Yomiuri Weekly* noted, "Kimura would win if it was a serious match, but Rikidōzan would win if it was merely a show." [25] Rikidōzan was incensed when he read this, and screamed his displeasure at the editorial office.

The nation was on the edge of their seats when the gong sounded. Kimura and Rikidōzan followed the script, with both wrestlers throwing each other repeatedly. However, things took an unexpected turn when Rikidōzan made a slight appeal that one of Kimura's kicks landed in the groin. Reacting impulsively, Rikidōzan delivered powerful straight right to Kimura's jaw. He then continued with a series of

---

24 The third highest professional sumo rank after Yokozuna and Ozeki.
25 *The Yomiuri Weekly* (10 December 1954) pp. 18–20

An historic victory. Rikidōzan triumphs over Kimura in a legendary showdown, cementing his legacy in wrestling history. Kimura has been knocked to the ground and is on the verge of unconsciousness following an unscripted barrage of kicks and punches to the head and neck.

sumo-style slaps, eventually knocking Kimura to the mat. As Kimura attempted to sit up, Rikidōzan escalated the assault by kicking him in the face with the toe of his wrestling shoe, stomping on the back of his head, and striking a right-handed chop to his neck arteries. Finally, a vicious left-handed slap to the jaw left Kimura temporarily unconscious, resulting in a KO loss.

A pool of blood stained the mat. Fans of judo were heartbroken as they witnessed Kimura, their absolute hero, fall so unceremoniously in defeat on national television.

Five Great Takudai Martial Artists

Testimony – Miyazawa Masayuki, Takudai Wrestling Team

"After graduating from Takudai, I worked for the *Tōkyō Shinbun* newspaper before joining *Nikkan Sports* in June 1954. Six months later, I was assigned to cover the fight between Kimura Masahiko and Rikidōzan. Most newspapers sent a department head to cover the spectacle, but since I was Kimura's junior at Takudai, I was given the job even though I was a rookie. When I met Mr. Kimura, I said OSU. He responded in kind.

The match was a complete disaster, and even the big newspapers like *Asahi*, *Yomiuri*, and *Tokyo* announced their immediate withdrawal from pro wrestling after seeing the brutal outcome.

The next day, I went to the Chiyoda Hotel in Kand-abashi with a cameraman to visit Mr. Kimura, who was clearly in a lot of pain and had a terribly swollen face. I didn't feel right about requesting a photo given his condition, but since the company had tasked me with the job, I mustered up the courage to ask anyway.

'Miyazawa,' he said, 'if you want to take a picture, take it from this side.' OSU, I replied. Mr. Kimura added, 'It's over. You can't temper the arteries in your neck to withstand a pounding like that, you know.' I was impressed with his demeanor. Then, Ōyama Masu-tatsu entered the room. Ōyama declared emphatically. 'OSU Kimura-senpai, I'll take care of the bastard with my karate!"

Kimura Masahiko, visibly injured and defeated, following his iconic wrestling match against Rikidōzan. This rare moment captures a legend facing one of his few setbacks in an otherwise illustrious career in combat sports. The headline reads "Swells of a Mortal Combat."

The following is what Miyazawa wrote in the *Nikkan Sports* quoting Kimura.

> "Using punches to take down an opponent in a wrestling match isn't true to the sport; That's more like boxing. If you're going to punch, you might as well be in a boxing ring against a top American heavyweight. I had some experience with karate during my student days, and I can vouch for the effectiveness of Ōyama's

techniques like *nukite* (spear hand) and *shutō* (knife hand). He's even defeated several wrestlers in the US with his karate skills. Now, he's eager for a chance to face Rikidōzan, hoping to get his shot before Yamaguchi Toshio does. I can predict how that match would end."[26]

Rikidōzan never faced Ōyama or Kimura after that and continued to reign as professional wrestling ace. He trained many successors, including Giant Baba[27] and Antonio Inoki,[28] and contributed much to the establishment of the pro wrestling business in Japan. In December 1963, he got into a fight with *yakuza* in a nightclub over some trivial matter, and was stabbed with a knife. He died as a result of his injuries at the age of 39.

Kimura's life took a few twists and turns following the Rikidōzan affair, but he eventually found his footing as a lecturer in Takushoku University's Physical Education Department, and became the Shihan of the Judo Club in 1961. In fact, Doug Rogers, the Canadian heavyweight who won a silver medal at the 1964 Tokyo Olympics, specifically came to Takudai to seek guidance from Kimura. Impressed by Rogers' skills, Kimura extended an invitation to him to join the university and help train and compete for the judo team. Together, they led the Takudai team to victory in the All-Japan Student Judo Championships.

A documentary by the National Film Board of Canada titled "Judoka" (1965) chronicles Roger's life in Japan and can be viewed on YouTube. The footage shot in 1965 provides an interesting

26 *Nikkan Sports* (24 December 1954)
27 1938–1999. Japanese professional wrestler, professional baseball player, founder of All Japan Pro Wrestling, and one of the so called "Big Three" in Japanese professional wrestling along with Rikidōzan and Antonio Inoki.
28 1943–. Japanese professional wrestler, businessman, and politician. Founder of New Japan Pro-Wrestling. Was scouted by Rikidōzan during a tour of Brazil and became a professional wrestler. See Chapter 6.

glimpse of his life in Japan. It also contains rare footage of Kimura, and Iwatsuri Kaneo,[29] captain of the team.

At the end of practice, everyone kneels in *seiza*. After the captain gives the order to "bow to the sensei!" the members prostrate from the seated position while shouting OSU in unison to Shihan Kimura. After the next command, "Bow to the *shōmen!*" (altar at the front) they all lower their heads in silence. OSU is directed only at the master.

In 1899, the Dai-Nihon Butokukai built the Butokuden dojo near Heian Jingū Shrine in Kyoto. Martial arts demonstrations have been held there regularly ever since. In accordance with ancient Chinese protocols which were adopted by Japan, the emperor faces the south while governing. Thus, the north side of the Butokuden is regarded as the *shōmen*, and the emperor's throne is in the center. The order "bow to the *shōmen*" (the throne, i.e., His Majesty) became an established part of the budo etiquette in Japan. It is from this line of thought that people pay silent reverence to the "front" of the dojo.

5. World-Famous Kanazawa Hirokazu

The founder of the Shotokan Karate-do International Federation, Kanazawa Hirokazu, dedicated his life to promoting karate and OSU around the globe (SKIF usually writes it as OSS rather than OSU). His efforts saw him traveling to over 120 countries, where he taught karate to eager students, sharing his wisdom and passion for the martial art. Although Kanazawa passed away in 2019, his legacy lives on and his teachings continue to inspire and motivate karate enthusiasts worldwide.[30]

---

29 1944–2011. Kimura's number one student at Takudai and 1971 All Japan Judo Champion.
30 1931–2019. Winner of the 1st National Karatedo Championship held in 1957. Founder of the Shotokan Karatedo International Federation (SKIF).

Kanazawa Hirokazu (1931–2019) was a distinguished Japanese Shotokan karate master who was instrumental in karate's international dissemination. He held the position of Chief Instructor and President of the Shotokan Karate-Do International Federation, an organization he established following his departure from the Japan Karate Association (JKA). Kanazawa achieved the highest honor in his discipline, being awarded the 10th dan rank in Shotokan Karate. He was a direct student of Funakoshi Gichin.

The Takudai Karate Club has played a central role in the spread of karate globally, and by extension of this, OSU. As I have already outlined, this has a lot to do with Takudai's culture and motto of sending graduates abroad to forge new pathways. Former members of Takudai's karate club certainly lived up to this ideal, and then some.

Kanazawa was a true trailblazer in promoting karate internationally. Through his teaching and demonstrations in numerous countries, he laid the groundwork for the widespread adoption of karate and ensured that his labors would be carried forward by his successors. His efforts were instrumental in making karate a well-recognized and highly respected discipline worldwide.[31]

I interviewed Master Kanazawa, known in Japan as "the World's Kanazawa," about OSS and how it was disseminated internationally.

— *How many countries have you taught in so far?*
"During my career, I have had the honor of traveling to over 120 countries to teach karate, extending my influence far beyond direct interactions. Although there are nearly 60 countries in Africa, I have visited only 12, yet I've met many dedicated students. Some of these students traveled long distances, enduring grueling journeys by bus and train for up to two weeks, just to attend my three-day seminars.

My travels have also led to many unique encounters. I've met various people who identify as followers of Kanazawa karate, Kanazawa-ryū, or Shotokan Karate-do International. I've been asked to autograph pirated copies of my books and once met an African karateka who introduced himself as Kanazawa Hirokazu!"

— *Is OSS a prevalent term in all of these countries?*
"Yes, it's used a lot. Whenever I go to some country to teach karate, the first thing I do is explain OSS."

— *Were you instructed by the Japan Karate Association to teach the meaning of OSS overseas?*

---

31 Kanazawa's fascinating autobiography was translated into English in 2003 by Alex Bennett. H. Kanazawa, *Karate My Life* (Nippon Budokan, 2003)

"No such directive was ever forthcoming. Budo, the Japanese martial ways, focus on achieving unity of the mind and body, with the ultimate goal of cultivating character through physical training. It's not just about winning competitions, but about discovering one's limitations and overcoming them. This philosophy is captured by the essence of OSS, a term I use with pride.

That's why I try to convey the spirit of OSS outside Japan as well. I teach how the term is supposed to be used. That is, when bowing to the teacher or fellow students and the like, but not when bowing before the gods, to the dojo's *shōmen*, or the national flag. The Japan Karate Association, established with the help of Takudai Karate Club old boys like Nakayama-sensei, is largely responsible for the widespread use of OSS today. However, we were already using it well before the association's formation. And now, I've adopted the habit of signing off my letters with OSS – it just comes naturally to me!"

— *During your time at Takudai, was OSS used outside the karate club as well?*
"Most students belonged to some kind of club, so everyone used it, not just the cheering squad or athletic clubs. I learned it from my seniors when I joined the karate club. They'd drive home to us that 'Takudai equals OSS!'"

— *Have you ever heard of the teaching "Endure the unendurable, suffer what is not sufferable. Push when pushed, push when pulled. This spirit of self-denial is the spirit of OSS?*

"Yes, of course. From my college days. Everybody knew this."

— *I hear that at Takudai, OSS means "me," "you" and various other things. Was this the case when you were there?*
"Yes, there were many people who used OSS this way. Actually, I think most of them were from Kyushu. Come to think of it, there were heaps of students from Kyushu at Takudai back then."

— *Have you ever heard the theories that OSS came from Hagakure, or that it arose at the Naval Academy?*
"When I first enrolled at Takudai, one of the senior members told me that OSS had its roots in the Naval Academy. To my surprise, I also heard some claim the term originated in the *Hagakure*, a famous book on samurai culture. Maybe someone from Saga Prefecture, where the *Hagakure* was written, came up with this theory on a whim. Or maybe they were just trying to impress their friends with some fancy samurai trivia."

— *What are some of your memories from teaching abroad?*
"Back in my Hawaii days, I had to deal with a bunch of 'dojo breakers' who fancied themselves as martial arts hotshots. These clowns included karate fighters, wrestlers, boxers, and other tough guys who thought they could take me down a peg or two. I must've dealt with at least twenty of them, and some of these bozos kept coming back for more even after I refused their challenges. Let me tell you, even if you beat a local in a street fight, it's not going to do you any favors. I ended up taking on four of them in the end, but I'll spare you the gory details.

But that wasn't the only crazy thing I encountered. In some countries, I ran into folks who refused to bow to the *shōmen* or sensei out of religious reasons. They'd kneel in *seiza* like everyone else, but when it came to lowering their heads to show respect, they'd be like 'nah, God's the only one I'm bowing to.' Can't argue with that, I guess.

Then there were dojos with the country's flag displayed alongside the Rising Sun. One guy asked me why an American should bow to the flag of Japan since the Japs lost the war? I had to set him straight and explain the whole respect imperative. He apologized later, so I guess I got through to him.

Now, speaking of Hawaii, I once did a demo with Mas Ōyama. I knew him from way back when my brother and I saw him fight a bull in Tateyama, Chiba. Good times. Anyway, I organized a 'Hawaii Karate Congress' and put on a show. I smashed two boards in midair with a kick and a punch, and Ōyama-sensei chopped the top off a beer bottle. Back then, karate was known as 'Empty Hand,' which always makes me laugh because it's useful when you don't have a bottle opener."

— *What does OSS mean to you?*

I believe that the word OSS expresses the spirit of perseverance, effort, and achievement, which means that no matter what difficulties you come across, you do not give up. You persevere and ultimately achieve your goal.

OSS is more than just a nifty phrase to shout out every chance you get. It embodies the spirit of never giving up, no matter how hard life kicks you in the face. It's not meant to be thrown around like confetti or used as a quick fix solution. You gotta mean it, man. Speaking of which, have you noticed how impatient people are these days? It's like everyone's in such a hurry they forget to take a breath and slow down. We could all use a little more OSS in our lives, if you ask me.

(March 30, 2016 at the Honbu Dojo of the Kokusai Shotokan Karate-do Federation.)

Kanazawa Hirokazu meditates quietly during a trip to Peru.

Column 3: 押 and 忍 in Classical Japanese Literature

The *Kojiki* (Records of Ancient Matters, c. 712), *Nihon Shoki* (Chronicles of Japan, c. 720),[1] and *Man'yōshū* (c. 759) are representative books of ancient Japan. They were completed during the Nara period (710–794). This column will outline the prevalence of the *kanji* 押 and 忍 found in these texts.

Ame-no-Oshihi-no-Mikoto (天忍日命, also written as 天押日命), a deity mentioned in *Kojiki*, was the ancestral god of the Ōtomo clan. Arai Hakuseki[2] wrote in his etymology book Tōga (1717), "There are many names for imperial princes, such as Oshi (押) and Oshi (忍)." Indeed, in the *Kojiki* and *Nihon Shoki* explanations imperial lineage, these two *kanji* often feature in the titles of ancient Japanese emperors and members of the imperial family. The sixth emperor Kōan's son, for example, is named Ame-Tarashihiko-Kunioshihito-no-Mikoto (天足彦国押人命) in the *Nihon Shoki*, but is written as 天足彦国忍人命 in other sources. In the *Man'yōshū*, "oshiteru" is used as a pillow word[3] to praise the land of Naniwa.[4] It is written as 押照 in Volume 4, and 忍照 in Volume 16, and can be translated as "Far Shining Naniwa."

In volume 8 of the *Kojiki-den*, a commentary on the *Kojiki* that took Motoori Norinaga[5] 35 years to finish, it is stated that 押 and 忍 (oshi) were not words to be used flippantly as they were once titles of respect and reverence. In volume 21 of this work, there is also a reference to the interchangeability of 押 and 忍. In the *Nihon Shinmei Jiten* (Dictionary of Japanese Divine Names), 押 and 忍 are defined as "the aesthetic name for something that has divine power." The *Sumō Dai-jiten* (Sumo Encyclopedia) says, "In the world of sumo, 忍 has the same meaning as 押 and means to push." The ancient Shinto rituals that are performed in sumo are surely connected with this usage.

---

1 Considered to be the first imperial history book in Japan. It describes events from the divine era to the year 697.
2 1657–1725. A Confucian scholar, bureaucrat and politician during the mid-Edo period.
3 A word that modifies or sets the tone before a predetermined phrase in *waka* poetry.
4 Osaka's representative downtown area today.
5 Motoori Norinaga (1730– November 1801) was a prominent Japanese Kokugaku (nativist) scholar during the Edo period.

CHAPTER 5

OSU and Upheaval

Ōendan

How did OSU make its way from Takudai to the rest of the world? There were two primary paths. The first was a vertical route through karate, which allowed the term to spread among generations of practitioners worldwide. The second was a horizontal route from Takudai to other university *ōendan* and karate clubs throughout the country. This route peaked from the 1960s to the 1980s. But what is an *ōendan*, you may wonder?

Cheering at sports events is a universal practice, with fans rallying behind their teams to motivate and support the athletes toward victory. In Japan, this role is often filled by specialized squads known as *ōendan*. Comparable to cheerleading teams in the USA, *ōendan* serve a similar purpose in boosting team spirit and energizing crowds. However, their approach differs significantly. *Ōendan* typically involve highly coordinated group chants and complex rhythmic routines, emphasizing unity and precision, reflecting traditional aspects of Japanese culture in their performance style.

The Japanese college *ōendan* are conservative, male-dominated groups with strict hierarchies and harsh training regimes designed to cultivate a strong sense of solidarity and service. Members are pushed to their limits through rigorous drills that are reminiscent of hardcore martial arts training, with upperclassmen providing strict 'encouragement' to their charges to sweat more, bleed more, and challenge their physical endurance.

Cheering squads were not originally part of college sports in Japan. They emerged organically as members of athletic clubs and ordinary students came together to support their school teams. In the prewar period, these spontaneous supportergroups eventually formalized their activities, establishing structured clubs dedicated solely to attending sporting events. Their aim was to lift the spirits of both the athletes and the supporting student body. These clubs developed into what are known today as *ōendan*, characterized by their regimented, spirited displays that are a staple at sports events across Japanese schools and universities.

Katō Shū was the first president of the All-Japan Student Ōendan Federation, which was formed in 1951. According to Katō, *ōendan* customarily had the following traits:

> "Cheering squads were originally created out of necessity, with the goal of helping university teams win sports competitions. The *ōendan* mentality is rooted in the desire to help athletes demonstrate their full potential. It's all about supporting others, not hogging the limelight for yourself. The *ōendan* spirit is all about feeling a sense of relief and joy when the athlete shines.
>
> Being a part of an *ōendan* means putting yourself last. Before the war, the groups weren't as organized as they are today, and the appellation *ōendan* wasn't

The Meiji University ōendan supporting their team at a baseball game. Like a conductor, the leader is standing at the front giving cues to the cheering squad members and brass band to the left. The flag-bearer typically holds the heavy standard for the entirety of the match. This requires immense stamina and willpower, especially under the hot summer sun.

even in use. Historically, the role of *ōendan* leaders was reserved for those who were physically strong or skilled in fighting. This was partly because if a team lost a game, the typical response from the *ōendan* was to confront and physically challenge the opposing cheering squad. Such encounters aimed to outmatch the rival *ōendan* through direct confrontation. Consequently, any happening on the baseball field, in the boxing ring, or in the judo hall could trigger a brawl among the *ōendan* members, reflecting a more aggressive and combative aspect of school sports culture during that era..."[1]

The ability and charisma to unite the crowd as well as the capacity to break up fights (or, prevail in) were called for, so people with an audacious disposition tended to fall into this role. This temperament became firmly entrenched in the culture among the members of later *ōendan*.

Ōendan members were (and still are) characterized by a distinctive style known as "*bankara*," in which students wear outmoded Japanese *haori* and *hakama* or black Prussian-styled school uniforms (*gakuran*), school caps, and high wooden clogs (*geta*). This purposefully passé appearance denotes a rough-and-ready, righteous and anti-establishment attitude.

Ōendan contribute to the formation of a sense of order on campus, not only by cheering for the athletic teams, but also as a centripetal force for all students by supporting the university community. In the *ōendan*, it is considered more important to observe traditional customs, maintain iron discipline, and adhere to stringent hierarchical relationships than abide by more rational or efficient methods.

---

1 *Zen Nihon Gakusei Ōendan Renmei Keidan Renmei 25 Shūnen Kinen-shi* (25th Anniversary of the Formation of the All-Japan Student Ōendan Federation, 1976) p. 15.

The *ōendan* does not boast a celebrated record like the athletic teams it turns out for. It serves as a shadowy presence cheering for any victory to honor its alma mater.

Like athletes of sports teams, however, members train extremely hard to cultivate a robust body and mind. Their sense of belonging to the university is fostered through their exacting, often cruel practices, which eventually sublimates into blind love for their school not unlike unbridled nationalism. The *ōendan* is usually a group of men (very few women belong to these groups) who give their all, and give up everything for their school.

In the prewar period when karate competitions had yet to be developed, college karate club members often doubled as members of cheering squads. The *ōendan* had their own special *kata* (choreographed forms). This is why karate *kata* and techniques such as the *shōken-tsuki* punch are incorporated into *ōendan* routines to this day. Thus, karate clubs and cheering squads conventionally have a strong affinity with each other.

For example, Nakayama Masatoshi at Takushoku University, and Yamaguchi Gōgen, founder of the karate club at Ritsumeikan University also served as the respective heads of their university *ōendan*. Katō Shū was also the manager of Nihon University's karate team. The standard *kata* of Meiji University's *ōendan*, however, was based on the *shiranui-gata* movements from sumo,[2] since the first leader of the squad, Soma Motoi (1896–1981), was also a member of the sumo club. In any case, martial arts and *ōendan* go hand in hand.

---

2 One of the *kata* performed by Yokozuna grand champions in professional sumo when they enter the ring.

Nakayama Masatoshi cuts a striking figure, impeccably dressed in his traditional haori and hakama, complete with a cane and a classic school cap. Known for his mastery in karate, here Nakayama is captured in his distinctive ōendan attire, exuding the spirit and elegance of a bygone era.

The Revival of Budo — The Martial Ways of Japan

From the 1960s to the 1980s, OSU usage peaked among college students in Japan. What of the historical background underlying this phenomenon?

Following defeat, Japan consequently relinquished its hold on the Korean Peninsula, Manchuria, and other outlying areas. After the economic and social devastation and chaos experienced in the aftermath of the war, Japan finally regained its independence from the Allied occupation with the signing of the San Francisco Peace Treaty in 1951. During the 18 years from 1955 to 1973, the economy grew at an average annual rate of just over 10%, and the Gross National Product more than quadrupled. This was remarkable growth, unprecedented in the world.

On October 1, 1964, the Tōkaidō Shinkansen, Japan's first high-speed Bullet Train railroad, opened for business. This signified the birth of an epoch-making transportation network. The Tokyo

The Nippon Budokan, a symbol of Japan's martial arts heritage, stands majestically as a venue dedicated to the promotion of traditional budo and a landmark for major cultural events. It was built in 1964 as the venue for judo's debut in the Olympic Games held in Tokyo that year. It is both a building and also a foundation promoting budo domestically and internationally.

Olympic Games were held in the same month and served to restore the wounded pride of the Japanese people on the world stage. It demonstrated that the country had recovered from defeat and was now a peaceful, prosperous nation.

As Japan achieved what was heralded as a "miraculous recovery," budo was also resurrected from the ashes. Budo was prohibited in the early postwar years due to its affiliation with wartime militaristic education. The Ministry of Education lifted its blanket ban on budo activities in schools incrementally. Judo resumed in 1950, followed by kyudo (archery) the following year. A tamer version of kendo was reinstated in schools in 1952 under the name of "*shinai kyōgi*" (pliant staff play).

The culmination of budo's reintegration into society as "modern democratic sports" came with the completion of the Nippon Budokan, a giant martial arts hall and umbrella organization for Japanese budo in central Tokyo in 1964. Its establishment was made possible with strong backing from the Japanese government.

"On June 5, 1961, Shōriki Matsutarō,[3] a member of the House of Representatives, gathered 46 members of the Diet and 17 experts in judo and kendo, and iterated the following three aspirations:

1. The spirit of budo is the foundation of the national spirit of Japan, and the Diet should actively promote it.
2. In the future, judo and kendo should be made official subjects of study in junior and senior high schools.
3. To achieve this goal, a world-class martial arts complex with a capacity of over 30,000 people should be

3 1885–1969. Bureaucrat, police officer, media mogul and politician.

built in the center of Tokyo.

With agreement from all present, construction of the
Nippon Budokan was decided."[4]

On September 15, 1964, less than a month before the Tokyo Olympics, construction of the Nippon Budokan was concluded. The
Budokan was unveiled as the venue for judo, the first Asian sport
to be adopted as an Olympic event. It was also the first time the
Olympics were held in an Asian country. It was a truly historic event
for Japan and judo.

Spartan Age of Discipline, Perseverance, and Spirituality

The Tokyo Olympics gave birth to the mentality in Japanese the
sports world that "if you have *konjo* (guts and the mental strength
to endure hardship), you can prevail."The *konjo* ideal influenced not
only top athletes but also school sports and athletic club activities. A
task force organized in 1961 for strengthening athletes for success
in the Tokyo Olympics formulated "*konjo* building" as an exclusive
program for priming Japan's sportsmen and women to win medals.
It even came to be thought of as a spiritual pillar of the Japanese
people enabling remarkable economic growth.

In 1965, the serialization "Kyojin no Hoshi"(Star of the Giants),
a masterpiece manga about baseball took Japan by storm. The pro-
tagonist endures immense hardship and overcomes all manner
of adversity through blood, sweat and tears, and an indomitable
spirit. Many other manga series and books related to *konjo* in sports
became bestsellers.

The *konjo* trend was prevalent not only in boys' manga but also
in those produced for girls. In 1968, "Attack No. 1" and "Sign as V,"

---

4 *Budo: The Martial Ways of Japan* (Nippon Budokan, 2011) p. 119.

both based on volleyball and marketed for girls, were so fashionable that they were later made into successful TV series. *Konjo* was a genderless concept seen as representing all that made Japan great.

In the mid-1960s, a wave of "baby boomers," born during the post-war period of high birth rates, entered college. This era, unfortunately, also saw a rise in violent incidents among students, bringing the issue of *shigoki*, or hazing, to the forefront of public discourse. As these new generations filled the college halls, the dynamics within student groups, including *ōendan* and other college organizations, became more complex and sometimes contentious. This led to increased scrutiny and discussion about the practices of hazing and its impact on campus life. Still, most of it went unchecked in the shadows.

People also started to feel like something was missing in their lives. This led to a rise in spiritual ideals, including *konjo*, which became increasingly popular among students. Many believed that *konjo* was a quintessential part of the Japanese psyche. In 1969, Ishihara Shintarō's book *Spartan Education* was published by Kōbunsha, and it quickly became a bestseller, moving over 700,000 copies.[5] The book was similar to popular sports manga of the time, promoting the virtues of discipline, courage, mental toughness, and a "Spartan attitude" towards life.

"University Troubles"

In 1968, in the lead up to renewing of the United States-Japan Security Treaty, a nationwide storm of university protests erupted, giving birth to the leftist All-University Joint Struggle League (Zengaku Kyōtō Kaigi).[6] The movement spread across the country

---

5 1932–2022. Japanese writer and politician. His younger brother is the actor Ishihara Yūjirō.
6 An anti-government, anti-U.S. movement mobilized to oppose ratification of this agreement. Mass demonstrations took place in 1970 and involved Diet members, workers, students, and citizens opposed to the Japan-U.S. Security Treaty. There was a swell in membership of leftist

*Japanese students in the late 60s captured during intense protests, reflecting a tumultu-
ous period marked by their vigorous demand for political change and university reform.
Their actions symbolize a pivotal moment in Japan's post-war history, as young activists
sought to reshape societal norms and influence government policies.*

like wildfire. Right-wing forces were organized to confront the left, while both resisted various elements of government authority. The mainstay of the rightists were members of university budo clubs, *ōendan*, and right-wing student groups. They regularly set about intimidating their far more numerous left-wing student activist counterparts, and fierce confrontations ensued at flashpoints throughout the country.

Testimony – Yamazaki Terutomo

"In April 1968, I entered Nihon University (Nichidai). However, two months later, in June, the 'Nichidai Tōsō' student movement[7] began, and the university was closed. As I didn't know when classes would start up again, and couldn't return home, going to the dojo was the least expensive way to bide my time. A year after I entered the university, I founded the Nihon University Kickboxing Club so I could research fighting techniques. At the same time, I decided to devote my student life to karate until graduation.

During the Nihon University struggle, ideological divisions sharply delineated the campus, with leftists on one side and rightists on the other. Budo clubs at the university generally consisted of students with right-wing sympathies. In this charged atmosphere, I mobilized students from budo clubs to participate in security operations off-campus, such as at Narita Airport, which was still under construction. The airport's construction was a hotbed of controversy and a focal

---

and new-leftist groups which rallied against the treaty and other causes.
7 The turmoil at Nihon University that lasted from 1968 to 1969.

point of left-wing opposition [especially as the land had been commandeered off farmers].”

Right and left-wing students at this time were bitter enemies, but as they were all from the generation born just after the war, they shared a common trait in that they were staunch idealists. The students on the right supported a more nationalistic approach to government, while leftist students sought to undermine it. The two sides faced off across barricades and engaged in rancorous skirmishes nationwide.

From the 1960s to the 1980s, there were numerous right-wing student organizations. Some of them emerged during the university struggles, some were active before then, and some sprung up afterwards. Still, they all had things in common: they were disturbed by the society's tendency toward frivolity, they opposed communism, were highly patriotic, sang military songs, and honored their alma maters with zealous chauvinism. Members of these groups habitually used OSU.

OSU became not only a symbol of *konjo* and spiritedness, but also a word that took on elements of hierarchy and absolute obedience in order to enforce organizational discipline. At this time, university cheering squads, members of karate and other budo clubs, and right-wing students donned the priest-like garb of the *gakuran* uniform of matching black trousers and a tunic with a standing collar and gold buttons. These uniforms were modeled on the Prussian Waffenrock and were introduced into Japan in the 1880s. Although still seen in Japan today in some boys' schools (and college *ōendan*), the heyday of the *gakuran* coincided with the zenith of OSU usage at Japanese universities. The *gakuran* and OSU came to convey a spirit of staunch Japaneseness, self-assertion, and idealism.

A gakuran is a type of traditional Japanese school uniform for boys. The term is derived from "gaku" meaning "study" or "student" and "ran" from "ranpuku," which is an abbreviation of the Dutch word "rampjaar," referring to a style of military jacket. The gakuran is typically characterized by its black or dark-colored fabric, upright collar, and a series of buttons aligned vertically on the front. It is commonly worn by male students in junior high and high schools in Japan, often paired with matching trousers and sometimes a cap. The design was inspired by European-style naval uniforms and became widely adopted in Japanese schools during the Meiji era.

Testimony - Nakayama Masatoshi

Nakayama Masatoshi, first Shihan of the Japan Karate Association, Takudai old boy and later faculty member, and director of the Takudai *ōendan*, was familiar with, and somewhat critical of, OSU usage before, during, and after World War II.

"At the beginning of each new school year, freshmen were often overwhelmed by the loud chorus of OSU shouts from upperclassmen in the schoolyard, beneath the fully blossomed cherry trees. It might seem odd, but even as a Takudai alumnus, I still find such scenes startling when I witness them today. Despite this practice of shouting OSU being a long-standing tradition at Takudai, most people are mistaken about its true meaning. I find it particularly troubling to hear students from other universities indiscriminately chanting OSU on the streets, a trend that became popular after the war. In this respect, at least Takudai students maintain a better understanding of the tradition. Though the origins of the word are somewhat unclear, OSU was frequently heard during my time at Takudai. It is said by some to have been introduced by a senior student from the Naval Academy who joined Takudai in 1926.

Originally, OSU was a term used extensively among students and wasn't as widely adopted outside Takudai as it is today. For Takudai students, it was a way to express affection and sincerity, rather than serving as a battle cry or a boisterous cheer. Unlike the current usage, it wasn't employed as a catch-all substitute for common expressions like 'good morning,' 'please,' 'yes,' or 'no.' It's a mistake to use OSU as a blanket term instead of taking the time to communicate more thoughtfully and appropriately.

Sincerity and patience are fundamental values for Takudai students. It is disrespectful to casually say OSU to a teacher or an upperclassman, especially while turning away from them. The priority should always be to greet them respectfully and express sincerity.

Furthermore, using OSU in a manner that demeans others or stirs agitation is highly inappropriate, and in such cases, it would be better to refrain from using it at all. For example, shouting OSU loudly without considering the surroundings can cause discomfort. A sincere OSU spoken in a subdued voice is more than adequate."[8]

Maybe this discrepancy in usage can be attributed to a generation gap, but it is interesting to note that usage of OSU differed depending on the era. Nakayama felt that OSU before and during the war encompassed the spirit of determination and nation-building, while the postwar OSU became empty and superficial cliché.

The Shorinji Kempo Ban on OSU

Ueno Kazuhiro trained at the headquarters of Shorinji Kempo in Tadotsu, Kagawa Prefecture, from 1975 to 1979. He wrote about a ban on OSU imposed by the organization because of the errant attitude of students in college Shorinji Kempo clubs.

"Sō Dōshin,[9] the founder of Shorinji Kempo, held high expectations for students, believing they would become future leaders of Japan. In the 1960s, he attended college tournaments and awarded certificates and other honors to those who performed well. How-

---

8 *Takushoku Daigaku Ōendan Danpō OSS*, April 13, 1966.
9 1911–1980. Japanese martial artist, religious leader, and founder of Shorinji Kempo.

Sō Dōshin was the founder of Shorinji Kempo, a martial art that combines physical techniques with philosophical teachings, which he established in 1947. Born Michiomi Nakano, he developed this system based on his experiences in China, aiming to promote personal growth and social improvement. Sō Dōshin believed that fostering strength and compassion in individuals could lead to a more peaceful and cooperative society.

ever, by the 1970s, the focus of tournaments shifted towards violent sparring (*randori*) and winning by any means necessary. *Randori* was a type of boxing that involved gloves and a kendo body protector (*dō*), with fighters aiming to punch their opponent in the face or kick their torso. During matches, spectators would scream out such taunts as 'kill him,' and *senpai* would chasten their juniors if they lost.

In the 1960s and 1970s, nearly 10,000 students a year visited the head temple for training camps. In those days, many students wore oversized *gakuran* uniforms and they all said OSU a lot. OSU and *gakuran* came as a set. Sō Dōshin was very open-minded and tolerated the use of OSU even though it was not considered a greeting in Shorinji Kempo. He cared more about the spirit of the students."

At that time, OSU in Shorinji Kempo was a term utilized only by university students and not by ordinary members. In the mid-1970s, there was a spate of unfortunate deaths among college Shorinji Kempo club members due to violent *randori*, hazing (*shigoki*), and cruel punishments (*yaki*). Sō Dōshin was deeply troubled by this and ordered major reforms to the student federation in 1973.

Reforms included:
1. Prohibition of *randori* events at tournaments
2. Banning of baggy *gakuran* uniforms
3. No vocalization of OSU

Ueno goes into more detail:

"In the 1960s, the All-Japan Student Shorinji Kempo Federation was launched. Most college clubs were aligned with the original principles of Shorinji Kempo, which didn't have the same rigid hierarchical relationships as other budo clubs. However, by the early 1970s, things started to change. At tournaments, the *randori* division became increasingly brutal, and more and more students arrived at training camps wearing *gakuran* uniforms with exaggeratedly high collars and long hems....

Imperial Palace for Emperor Shōwa's birthday celebration. On May 10, the "Ōendan Jiken" (Cheering Squad Incident) ensued, in which a Takudai freshman died during a training camp. Takudai was harshly criticized by the media, and articles lambasting the school's culture were widely published.

The Cheering Squad Incident led to the resignation of President Toyoda Teisuke and the proclamation of a ban on wearing *gakuran* and using OSU. If a student was reprimanded for these infringements three times, it meant expulsion from the university. However, the problems persisted, and a little more than a month later, on June 24, the "Shinjuku Jiken" (Shinjuku Incident) transpired, with the university being condemned yet again in the media.

The Shinjuku Incident was a violent brawl that took place in Kabukichō,[11] involving Kokushikan University students and around 100 Takushoku University students who were holding a farewell party for their peers punished for the previous Cheering Squad Incident. The two universities handled the situation differently; Kokushikan took no action while Takudai expelled most of those involved. It was assumed that Takudai's meting out of severe punishment was due to the executive board's desire to eliminate the image associated with the uncouth "*bunkara*" style of students who were generating so much negative publicity.

The so-called "Committee for the Normalization of Takushoku University" was convened by concerned stakeholders and Iijima Isamu served as chairman. Iijima was 57 years old at the time. The following is the preface of a booklet dated August 15, 1978, that was distributed to Takudai students, faculty, staff, and alumni.

> "Takushoku University has implemented a ban on the use of the word OSU. Should a student utter the word three times, they face expulsion from the university.

11 One of the three major entertainment districts in Japan. Located in Shinjuku ward, Tokyo.

To improve the quality of Shorinji Kempo university clubs, the founder addressed the instructors during a training session in March, 1973. He expressed concern that many clubs were losing sight of the essence and origin of the art, and being influenced by bad habits prevalent in other college athletic clubs. He emphasized the importance of restoring etiquette and dress code to something more acceptable in the public eye. The use of OSU as a greeting and wearing high-collared, long-hemmed *gakuran* were no longer tolerated, as they were unsightly.

The founder also directed students to practice according to the regular Shorinji Kempo curriculum instead of focusing solely on *randori* and rough physical training. Upperclassmen were reminded to treat their juniors with respect, as *shigoki* and *yaki* were not in line with the philosophy of Shorinji Kempo.

He implored students to take the improvement of club activities seriously and added that even if the number of university clubs decreased, it wouldn't matter as long as the ones that remained returned to the original way of Shorinji Kempo. He threatened that clubs which failed to improve would be struck off."[10]

Takudai's OSU Ban

On the night of April 28, 1978, the "Kōkyo-mae Jiken" (Imperial Palace Incident) occurred, in which Kokushikan University students broke into the Takudai tent that had been erected in front of the

10 *Shōrinji Kempō Gojūnen-shi* (Shorinji Kempo Federation, 1997), p. 486.

参賀の泊まり込みで乱闘

国士館と拓大80人

二十八日夜、東京・皇居前広場で、天皇誕生日の参賀を泊まり込みで待っていた国士館大生グループが、拓殖大生グループに殴り込みをかけ、拓大生二人が十日のけがをする事件があった。

同日午後九時四十分ごろ、二重橋前広場で、拓大生約三十人が酒

館大生百二人と拓大生二十人を任意同行、首謀格の国士館大生六人を傷害、暴力行為の現行犯で逮捕、他の学生は取り調べ後、帰宅させた。現場のテント付近からはの一升ビン約三十本のほか、かんビール、つまみ、紙コップなどが散乱していた。

One of many newspaper articles detailing the fierce clash between the ōendan cheer groups of Kokushikan University and Takushoku University.

139

This policy has resulted in many students being reprimanded by university officials. This situation is absurd.

It is not clear when we first started saying OSU. According to one theory, it began when the greeting used by cadets in the Imperial Navy became popular among our student body. However, that does not seem to be the only reason. The two kanji 押忍 were assigned to the expression オス (OSU) after the war. 押忍 (OSU) might represent a part of what makes up the broader meaning of オス, but it is not entirely illustrative. Nevertheless, it is interesting to see how an aspect of Takudai's culture evolved after defeat to make 押忍.

For Takudai stalwarts (*Kōryō Kondei*), OSU means everything. At all times, all actions, joy, anger, sorrow, and pleasure are OSU... The reason why this masculine expression came to represent the Takudai loyalist's very soul is because the university has a history built on blood and sweat. Our predecessors martyred themselves without complaint for the preservation of the nation and the Asian cause. When we say OSU, we are heartened by our predecessors' sincerity, and are moved to our knees and ashamed to fall short of their expectations. We are proud of our Takudai culture. And we are happy to have an irreplaceable means of expressing the purist of souls. OSU."[12]

Iijima's proclamation triggered a movement to reform the university, and before long the OSU ban dissipated into thin air. OSU was back.

---

12 *"Kōryō Kenji yo Kōzen to Shite Hara no Soko Kara Osu wo Sakebe!"* pp. 1-2.

The End of Turbulent Times

From the 1960s to the 1980s, it was not unusual to see university *ōendan* with hundreds of members. Each cheering squad was fiercely competitive. Scandals were rife and became a much publicized social issue. Problems arose with the radicalization of some cheering squads. They engaged in activities far removed from supporting their sports teams, such as violent hazing and brawling with other *ōendan*. Such was the scale of the problems, several prestigious university *ōendan* were permanently discontinued.

During the 1990s, the traditional image of students wearing *gakuran* and shouting OSU in public and nightlife areas disappeared due to changes in student attitudes. Unlike the days when the hardcore "*bankara*" rough-and-ready student was 'respected' (or feared), brawling in that outdated, male-dominated world came to be considered archaic and very "uncool."

Karate club students stopped wearing *gakuran* and the hitherto hierarchical relationship between upper and lower classmen became more relaxed. Many *ōendan* folded due to a lack of membership, but those that survived changed their style of cheering by collaborating with brass bands and pompom-wielding cheerleader clubs made up entirely of women. *Ōendan* began to manage and conduct the support at sporting events, with brass bands providing a lively musical accompaniment and cheerleaders performing their acrobatic routines.

It might be unexpected for some to discover that cheerleading, a club activity deeply influenced by American culture, has integrated itself into *ōendan*, typically regarded as one of the most conservative club activities on Japanese university campuses. Nevertheless, this fusion has gradually become the standard for college cheerleading groups today.

Despite the significant decline in the number of *ōendan* members throughout Japan, the public's fascination with them remains strong. Even today, *ōendan* themes are popular in various media

Keeping Takudai traditions alive, Nakajima Takeshi is the quintessential Takudai OB. He is President of KIWA CORPORATION, Chairman of the Takudai Ōendan Alumni Association, and Chairman of the OSU Association.

such as manga, games, novels, movies, dramas, and TV commercials. There is an undeniable appeal to *ōendan* that still resonates with the Japanese people.

Column 4: Principal Aghast at OSU

In April 2015, a newly appointed principal at a junior high school was met by a boy in the corridor who greeted him with "Osssu." During the welcome speech, the principal expressed his disapproval of the greeting in front of the students. He called the student's action rude and threatened to physically discipline him. However, the school board reprimanded the principal the following day for his overreaction and he was required to apologize to students during another assembly.

Is OSU rude, or not? There were various opinions floating around the Internet regarding media reports on this little tiff. For example, if the student in question had bowed to the principal politely as he greeted him with OSU, he might have responded in turn instead of getting angry. However, if he was addressed with the more familiar *osu* instead of OSU, as if talking to a friend, then it is understandable why the principal would be offended. Although the difference might not be obvious to the ear, there is a subtle distinction in nuance between "*osu*" and "OSU." Using the latter to address someone who doesn't perceive it as polite can lead to incidents like this one in Japan. Not everybody does karate!

CHAPTER 6

The Internationalization
of OSU

Spreading the Word

Takudai graduates were dispatched around Taiwan, Korea, and Manchuria as "salt of the earth" protagonists of Asia in the prewar years. With Japan's defeat, however, the university's "founding spirit" was brought into disrepute, and the university itself was viewed with downright suspicion.

How was Takudai to survive in the new era and continue with its founding mission? There was no easy answer to this question, but stakeholders managed to find a solution of sorts through promoting emigration to Brazil and other countries in South America. Continuing in the tradition of the school's motto *Kaigai Yūhi* (Valiantly Crossing the Seas) graduate emigration began in the 1950s and reached its peak in the 1960s and 1970s. The flag of the Takudai *ōendan* fluttered daringly over the port of Yokohama, as students in *gakuran* uniforms bid their comrades *bon voyage*.

An emotional farewell. Takudai students wave goodbye to their upperclassmen embarking on a new journey to South America from Yokohama Port, marking the end of an era and the beginning of another.

Muhammad Hussain Inoki (originally born as Kanji Inoki on February 20, 1943, and passing on October 1, 2022) was a distinguished Japanese professional wrestler, martial artist, and politician. He also made significant contributions as a promoter of both professional wrestling and mixed martial arts. Widely recognized under the ring name Antonio Inoki, which he adopted as a tribute to the professional wrestler Antonino Rocca, Inoki achieved substantial acclaim as one of, if not the most popular and respected wrestlers in Japan.

The widespread popularity of OSU across the world owes a lot to the influence of these Takudai migrants and various martial arts styles they were connected to in some way, including Shotokan karate, Kyokushin Kaikan, Brazilian Jiu-Jitsu, judo, and Dutch kickboxing. These disciplines helped promote the use of OSU, which has also become synonymous with the performances of the world's best fighters in high-profile events such as UFC and K-1.[1] "Countless people in the Brazilian Jiu-jitsu community who use OSU," says Nakai Yūki, president of the Japan BJJ Federation.[2]

Takudai Karate Club alumni went to Brazil one after another in the 1950s. Among them was Kanazawa Hirokazu and his karate

---

1 A world-class kickboxing event founded in 1993 by Kazuyoshi Ishii, the founder of Seido Kaikan, a branch of the Kyokushin Ashihara Dojo.
2 1970–. The first "Shooto" World Welterweight Champion.

ABOVE AND RIGHT *On June 26, 1976, at the Nippon Budokan arena in Tokyo, Japan, a match dubbed "The War of the Worlds" took place under unique conditions that prefigured today's mixed martial arts (MMA). Throughout most of the bout, Inoki stayed on his back, taking advantage of a last-minute rule adjustment to kick Ali's legs 107 times without referee interference or risk of disqualification. The fight concluded in a draw, a result that sparked ongoing discussions and debates among journalists and enthusiasts.*

clubmate Sagara Juichi.[3] Born into a family of seven boys and four girls, one of Juichi's younger brothers was Antonio Inoki, the most famous professional wrestler in Japan.

Inoki fought with Mohammed Ali in 1976 resulting in a controversial draw.[4] The match billed as "The War of the Worlds" and considered by many as the precursor to MMA. The following is Inoki's recollection of emigrating to Brazil with family members in the 1950s.

> "It was around 1955 when we decided to go to Brazil. Cinemas were showing stirring movies set in the Brazilian jungle, as well as films featuring African beasts of prey. One day, my siblings and I went to see such a movie. My older brother Juichi, who was studying at Takushoku University, started telling us his dream. 'After I graduate, we should all go to Brazil. We'll cultivate a small area in the Amazon and build a little town there.' After a family meeting, it was decided that the brothers would not go alone. We would emigrate together with grandfather, mother, and eight brothers and sisters. Thus began our long 47-day boat trip in the spring of 1957. Whenever we got bored, Juichi would teach me karate on the deck."[5]

In 1968, Machida Yoshizō, father of former UFC light heavyweight champion Lyoto Machida, also went to Brazil. For a while, he worked as an instructor at Sagara Juichi's dojo in Sao Paulo.

---

3 1934–2001. Sagara was his mother's maiden name.
4 1942–2016. United States former professional boxer, former WBA and WBC unified world heavyweight champion, and one of the most famous boxers of the 20th century.
5 Antonio Inoki, *Otoko no Teiōgaku* (Wani Books, 1990), pp. 83–87

Testimony – Inoki Keisuke (Antonio Inoki's brother)

"My brother and I were thinking of going to the U.S. at first. However, at that time America did not accept Japanese immigrants. It was at the suggestion of Juichi that we decided to go to Brazil. If Juichi had not attended Takudai, our family would not have gone to Brazil, and the professional wrestler, Antonio Inoki, would not have been born. Lyoto Machida's father, Machida Yoshizō, lived in the same apartment with me when we first came to Brazil from Japan."

In 1968, Shōichirō Ogura was sent to Brazil as a Kyokushin Kaikan instructor.

Testimony – Ogura Shōichirō

"In 1967, after graduating from Takudai, I became an instructor at the Kyokushin Headquarters. The first instructor was Nakamura Tadashi, the second was Ashihara Hideyuki, and the third was Ōyama Shigeru. I became the fourth. A Nikkei bloke named Tanaka was running a Kyokushin dojo near São Paulo then. The Kyokushin head office received a request for an instructor. One year after I became an authorized teacher, Takudai graduate Iwafune Mitsugu, a senior member of the Brazilian Judo Federation, came to Kyokushin HQ and met me in the Director's office on the third floor. It was decided that I would go to Brazil. As it was to be my first trip overseas, the president of Kyokushin Kaikan, Ōyama Masatatsu, introduced me to someone through Kimura Masahiko who could advise me on what to do. When I taught in Brazil, I used Japanese words for technical terms such as *seiken* (knuckle punch) and *maegeri* (front kick), and of course OSU. This practice stemmed from my school days, I was always saying OSU in the dojo while I was at Takudai."

How and why did OSU come to be widely used in Brazilian Jiu-jitsu? Can it be traced to the dissemination of Shotokan and Kyokushin in Brazil? Alternatively, did it take root as a tribute to Japan, the mother country of *jūjutsu*? Whatever the case, there is no doubt that karate is deeply involved. Some Brazilian Jiu-jitsu dojos have even banned OSU on the grounds that "we are not karate!"

Still, it remains prevalent in BJJ. For example, Fabrício Werdum won the UFC heavyweight title unification fight in June 2015 and became undisputed champion. He said OSU at his interview after the weigh-in the day before. There is even an equipment brand called OSS Combat Sports.

OSU in Dutch Kickboxing

Ōnari Atsushi is a well-known kickboxing referee at events around the world. He said, "Kickboxers such as Peter Aerts, Remy Bonjasky, and Badr Hari typically use OSU as a greeting. Most kickboxers with a karate background, and there are many, say OSU."

Ernesto Hoost and Semmy Schilt set a remarkable record by winning the K-1 World Grand Prix four times each. The majority of K-1 World Grand Prix champions, including Peter Aerts, a three-time winner, and Remy Bonjasky, are associated with Dutch kickboxing gyms. Notably, Peter Aerts concludes his interviews with OSU. Endō Bunko, a martial arts journalist who lives in the kickboxing hub of the Netherlands, stated that OSU is predominantly used by martial artists associated with Kyokushin and kickboxing. Kyokushin made its way to the Netherlands in the 1960s, followed by kickboxing in the mid-1970s. He also mentioned that

Johannes Cornelius Bluming (1933 - 2018) was a prominent figure in the martial arts world, hailing from the Netherlands. He excelled as a martial artist, instructor, and actor, achieving high ranks with a 9th dan in Judo, 10th dan in Kyokushinkai Karate, and 10th dan in Hap-kido. Bluming was also known for his role as coach to Willem Ruska, who won two Olympic gold medals in judo.

Jon Bluming was the first to use it.

Jon Bluming is celebrated as one of the founders of the Dutch martial arts world. He was a judoka along with the legendary Anton Geesink.[6] He started karate in Japan at the Ōyama Dojo (predecessor of the Kyokushin Kaikan) in April 1959, while also training in judo at the Kodokan. After returning to the Netherlands in 1961, he established the Dutch branch of the Ōyama Dojo in Amsterdam and greatly contributed to the development of Kyokushin karate in Europe. Jon Bluming trained many fighters in both judo and karate.

Jan Kallenbach[7] and Loek Hollander[8] in karate. Willem Ruska[9] in judo. Chris Dolman[10] in sambo.[11] Kick-boxing's Jan Plas who

---

6 1934–2010. Gold medalist in the judo Open Division at the 1964 Tokyo Olympics.
7 1943–2021. Taikiken Kyōshi 7th Dan
8 1938–2020. Kyokushin 10th Dan.
9 1940–2015. Gold medalist in two weight classes at the 1972 Munich Olympics.
10 1945–. RINGS Holland representative.
11 A martial art developed in the Soviet Union.

trained Rob Kaman. Thom Harinck who trained Peter Aerts. Johan Vos who trained Ernesto Hoost. All of them are heavyweights in the Dutch martial arts world and have contributed to making the Netherlands a world-renowned powerhouse of combat sports.

In 1975, Jan Plas came to Japan to train in kickboxing under Kurosaki Kenji.[12] Kurosaki had previously taught karate to Jon Bluming. Plas returned to the Netherlands and created the Mejiro Gym Amsterdam, the first kickboxing gym in Europe.

At the Mejiro Gym Amsterdam, and in the gyms of Bob Schrijber and Jan Lomulder who had both trained there, they still follow Japanese dojo protocols of kneeling in *seiza* (formal sitting position) and *mokusō* (silent meditation) before and after practice. The orders are also given in Japanese. In addition, the instructor is called *sensei*, and the training system of Kyokushin karate is followed. The Kyokushin OSU has become well and truly ingrained in the Dutch kickboxing world.

OSU by Country

How is OSU used in various countries outside Japan? I interviewed several people to ascertain the extent of its spread.

Testimony – Honma Masahiko, New York Karatedo Honma Dojo

"To my knowledge, in the United States, the majority of Kyokushin practitioners use OSU. It's a simple word that can be easily pronounced by anyone, even those who don't speak Japanese. Personally, I greet my students' parents with OSU. When I teach Americans about the meaning of OSU at the dojo, I tell them

---

12 1930–. Mejiro Gym representative and former Ōyama Dojo teacher.

that it doesn't only mean endurance; it also means persist with humility. Additionally, I explain to children that it means 'I will try my best.'"

Testimony – Michael Dennis, South Carolina, Southeast Karate Association (Nanto Karate Kyokai)

"I was first introduced to OSU by my Sensei, Dana Burbank. He has been studying Shotokan karate since 1967. He received his first rank from Teruyuki Okazaki, but he primarily trained under Shigeru Takashina. He had the honor of training under JKA legends such as Masatoshi Nakayama, Masaaki Ueki, Takayuki Mikami, and many others who used OSU. We say OSU in our dojo the same way many others do (as a greeting, 'yes,' 'I understand,' etc.), but always with spirit! I consciously try to express OSU with a deeper meaning each time I say it. I understand OSU as an abbreviated version of 'osu no seishin' (the spirit of perseverance under pressure), pushing forward regardless of the obstacle in front of me. In my opinion, it serves as a much stronger motivator than 'ganbatte' (do your best), and stronger than the acknowledgment 'otsukare' (good work). In fact, that is a good way to describe OSU; it is strength, that inner strength you draw from when facing your toughest challenges. For me, it is the verbal expression of true warrior spirit. It is having the mindset that I will not be defeated or overcome by any adversity! OSU!"

Testimony – Nobukane Kazuhiko, International Karate-Do Gōjū-Kai Association Thailand Sakura Dojo

"Many of the students at my dojo are Japanese children. We greet each other in general Japanese. However, among the members of the Thailand Karate Federation, which consists of the Gōjū-kai and Japan Karate Association clubs, the common greeting is OSU.

Even though the body text in emails and SNS messages is in Thai, the concluding statement is always OSU. I explain the meaning of OSU as 'patience,' 'perseverance,' and 'endurance.' Thai karate was originally founded in 1964 by Nihon University College of Art Gōjū-ryū Karate Club graduate, Murakami Seiji. He is also my senior, and was asked to go to and teach karate in Thailand by Yamaguchi Gōgen, founder of the International Karatedo Gōjūkai Association. Although Gōjū-kai does not typically use OSU, our club was already using it in the 1960s.

Later, Ōmura Fujikiyo, a former member of the Takushoku University Karate Club and instructor of the Japan Karate Association, came to Thailand and further popularized it here. That's why Thai karate customs are strongly influenced by the traditions of Japanese university karate clubs. OSU is a good example."

The Nihon University College of Art Gōjū-Ryū Karate Club dates back to 1946. At the request of Mas Ōyama, the club was taught by instructors from the Ōyama Dojo. Jon Bluming, Yamazaki Terutomo, and others trained there. The famous actor Ishibashi Masashi, and Yamaguchi Gōshi, third son of Yamaguchi Gōgen and second president of the IKGA, also came from this esteemed club.

Testimony – Philip Sneyd, Masuda Dojo Ireland Kyokushin Kaikan

"OSU is a great way to say 'yes,' 'I understand,' and 'let's do our best!' etc. In Ireland, it is also used by practitioners of Brazilian Jiu-jitsu and judo. In our basic training, we go through the moves shouting '*Ichi!*' (1) then '*Sei!*' '*Ni*! (2) '*Sei!*' In the UK, Kyokushin dojos shout '*Ichi!*' '*OSU!*', '*Ni!*' '*OSU!*'… So, OSU is even bellowed out as *kiai*. I think it's a bit overused."

Testimony – Arthur Meek, England Wado-Ryu Karate-Do Academy

"In England, Shotokan, Gōjū-ryū, and Kyokushin styles say OSU, but we in Wadō-ryū don't use it at all. I was taught by master Shiomitsu Masafumi that OSU is not to be said as a greeting in our tradition."

Sandy A. Juhasz, a photojournalist who visited Japan to report on Japanese budo describes the situation in his native country. "In Hungary, OSU is used as a greeting by karate, kickboxing, and MMA athletes. There are two ways to write it: OSU or OSS, depending on your preference. Either way, it means good morning, thank you, good job, or well done, and you hear it all the time."

Chinese martial arts master Ji Long Zhao, host of "Real Kung Fu," a popular segment of the "Sports Online" broadcast on China Central Television, discusses the state of OSU in his country.

"I myself do not say OSU. Instead, I bow with my palms together in the traditional Chinese style. That said, OSU can be heard in China as well. For example, some of my students used to practice karate, and they often greet each other with OSU. In China, not only karateka but also Brazilian Jiu-jitsu practitioners use the term. Personally, I think that it has a positive connotation. It sounds plucky and stylish, and is a great ritual exchange between people. In China, the character for 忍 is seen more often than 押. You will often see large, handwritten calligraphy of 忍 framed and displayed in a karate dojo. I find this character to be more ascetically oriented. People who know nothing about Japan are oblivious to 押忍. Chinese who respect the culture and have established friendly relations with the Japanese find the word to be solemn and positive."

How did OSU Spread?

"When I tell people that I am a karate instructor overseas, Japanese people often ask me, 'Are you from Takudai?'" These are the words of Tokitsu Kenji, a long-time karate teacher in Paris. I interviewed him on May 5, 2015, during his temporary return to Japan.

"There are not many people from Hitotsubashi University Karate Club, my alma mater, who have become karate professionals. I think it's just me and Hamai Noriyasu of Kyokushin Kaikan. I'm currently teaching Jiseido, the martial art I founded in Europe. Most karate practitioners in France use OSU regardless of their style. Morning, noon and evening greetings are of course expressed as OSU. So too are goodbye, good night, thank you, and sorry. It's all basically Taku-dai-style OSU."

So how did OSU spread throughout the world of karate?

"When we think about why OSU has become so widespread, an unexpected factor in cultural transmission comes to mind. Outside Japan, often it is the case that martial arts like karate, judo, aikido, and kendo are not usually seen as separate practices, but rather as a collective part of Japan's traditional culture associated with the samurai. Karate is part of a larger cultural narrative of Japan, which includes martial arts, samurai, *kamikaze*, *harakiri*, *katana*, and Zen.

While Japanese people recognize the distinctions between budo such as karate, judo, and kendo, they also appreciate their broader ties to Japanese culture and the samurai ethos. However, it's worth noting that typical associations with budo do not usually include direct references to samurai, *seppuku*, or *kamikaze* suicide squads. Although a connection exists, it is generally considered tenuous in the modern sense. A distinction is made.

For foreign enthusiasts, however, the martial arts serve as a window into Japanese culture in general. And, they see traditional and modern culture associated with budo as one and the same... Also, I believe that OSU has become a symbol of belonging within the karate community, reflecting its status as a representative element of Japanese culture. In places like France, where OSU is not widely recognized by the general public, it essentially functions as a secret handshake among karate enthusiasts. When karate practitioners exchange OSU, they affirm their shared identity and connection through the discipline."

Talking with Tokitsu drew my attention to another trait of OSU. Could one of the reasons for the spread of OSU outside Japan be attributed to idea of *kotodama*? *Kotodama*, or "sacred sound" as it is sometimes translated into English, is a widespread Japanese belief that mystical powers dwell in words and names. Japanese would view the spread of OSU internationally as a demonstration of the power of *kotodama* in that it even resonates with the core of foreign martial artists who do not speak or understand Japanese.

It may seem strange and decidedly unscientific, but the straightforward, three-letter word "OSU" carries a unique aura. As we have seen, widely used by martial artists from diverse backgrounds, OSU often appears as a powerful sign-off in emails, social media posts, and letters. Whether expressing congratulations or offering condolences, OSU can communicate a broad spectrum of emotions effectively, as long as the underlying message is heartfelt. When used to conclude a message, it helps convey the sender's sincerity and earnestness. This single word has thus become a recognized symbol of authenticity within martial arts communities everywhere.

Takudai Mission Accomplished

Students at the Taiwan Association School, the predecessor of Takushoku University, were required to submit a written pledge stating their intentions to be posted overseas after graduation. Of course, this was in line with the school's motto *Kaigai Yūhi* (Valiantly Crossing the Seas) to faraway lands as "salt of the earth" migrants.

OSU has been embraced globally, owing to the contributions of renowned martial artists who trained at Takudai, and their successors. It is worth noting that OSU is more prevalent outside Japan than among the younger generation within.

Shioda Gōzō's Yōshinkan aikido has successfully amassed an international following, as has Kyokushin Kaikan karate, although it fragmented into different groups after the death of Mas Ōyama. The worldwide popularization of Shotokan karate was spearheaded by Nakayama Masatoshi and Kanazawa Hirokazu. Their tireless efforts ultimately led to karate becoming an Olympic event in 2021 at the Tokyo Olympiad.

The family of Hélio Gracie, who lost to Kimura Masahiko in a match in Rio, has continued their line of Gracie Jiu-Jitsu. It retains a more martial flavor than the highly regulated and competitive form of judo practiced in Japan. In any case, Takudai influence is always there somewhere, either directly or indirectly.

The third verse of the Takushoku University anthem declares, "There is no discrimination where I stand, based on color, race or birth land." Similarly, Takudai's OSU transcends such boundaries. It's astonishing that a term originating from one university in Japan has achieved such global resonance and buy-in, touching the lives of countless individuals across different cultures.

I sought the insight of Sasahara Hiroyuki, a respected Japanese *kanji* expert and professor at Waseda University, on this phenomenon. He pointed out that it is unheard of to find a word that captures the essence of a specific institution and goes on to gain global recognition. In his opinion, OSU is a term of immense influence, encapsulating deep thoughts and emotions. OSU is a truly unique word."

Takudai was founded with the goal of preparing individuals to make significant contributions to human progress in various fields internationally. Over a century after its establishment, Takudai still embraces its motto of *Kaigai Yūhi*. The term OSU has played a crucial role in helping the university achieve its mission, serving as a symbolic and practical tool in its educational endeavors. More so, however, OSU has become a word that unites tens of millions of people around the world for their shared love and respect of the martial arts. A single word, but a language unto itself.

A junior student at Takudai greets an upperclassman with an enthusiastic OSU. ("King" March, 1954)

Column 5: Oath and OSU

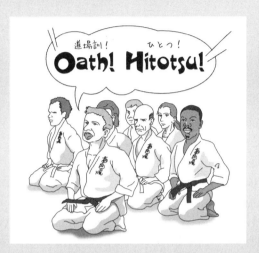

The English word "oath" has the same pronunciation as OSU, at least to the ear of a Japanese person. Making an oath is a solemn act and used in such ways as "an oath before God." In the Merriam-Webster Dictionary, oath is defined as "a solemn usually formal calling upon God or a god to witness to the truth of what one says or to witness that one sincerely intends to do what one says." In court of law, a person places his or her hand on a Bible and swears an oath. Oaths are made at important times in one's life, such as in a written pledge when starting work at a company, or promising "until death do us part" at a wedding.

When written in *katakana*, as loan words usually are in Japanese, oath (オース) sounds remarkably similar to OSU (オス). This is simply due to the fact that Japanese generally find it difficult to distinguish between "s" and "th" pronunciation. There is, of course, no direct connection between the words even though they do overlap in terms of solemnity.

Dojos in Japan and around the world often recite "*dōjō-kun*," or dojo oaths, which outline the expected behaviors and attitudes of their members. These oaths are affirmed through respectful bows before and after training sessions, and they are frequently displayed in prominent calligraphy on the walls of the dojo. Similarly, the word OSU was also an expression of the oaths made by those committed to rebuilding Japan after its defeat in World War II. In my opinion, the essence of "OSU" is deeply connected to the spirit of an "oath."

CHAPTER 6

Recap: The Evolution of OSU

Prewar and Wartime

OSU (オス) was first used by Takudai Sumo Club members. They adopted the term as a greeting to honor the sumo imperative of "pushing" (押し=oshi). It is completely different in meaning to the common greeting *ohayō gozaimasu* (good morning) which was/is often abbreviated to *osu*.

Before the war, Takudai's education focused on and colonial expansion. Based on its founding ideology, Takudai education sought to nurture individuals endowed with a temperament for "proactive advancement," and those prepared to "actively and willingly take action." The quintessence of sumo, "*osaba ose*" (endure when pushed), aligned perfectly with Takudai slogans like "Push through, and all will open up" and "Break new ground with a single push." Consequently, OSU became a unique greeting among Takudai students, not just the Sumo Club, symbolizing mutual regard for a common mission.

オス OSU
↓

Postwar

Amid the chaos of defeat and Japan's first occupation, and the humiliation of having to change the university's name from Takushoku University to Kōryō University, the characters 押忍 (OSU) were conceived by somebody at Takudai. This idea was inspired by the emperor's speech announcing Japan's surrender, which called for "enduring the unendurable, and suffering the unsufferable," and combining it with the fundamental sumo principle (push, endure).

押忍 OSU
↓

Modern Era

With the global spread of karate organizations such as the Japan Karate Association and Kyokushin Kaikan, OSU (OSS) has become a universal term. It has also spread to other martial arts and combat sports.

↓

OSU (OSS)

Martial Artist Connections

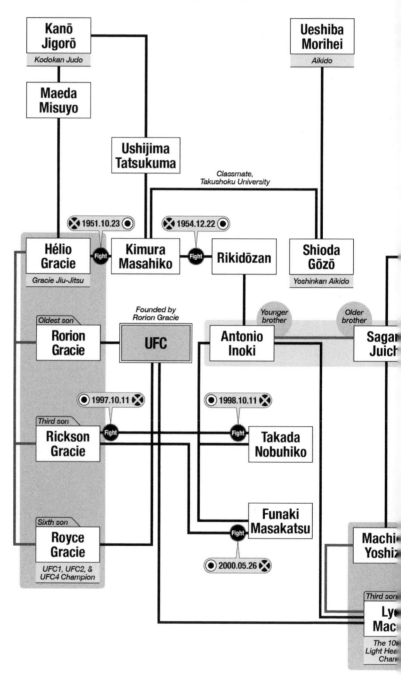

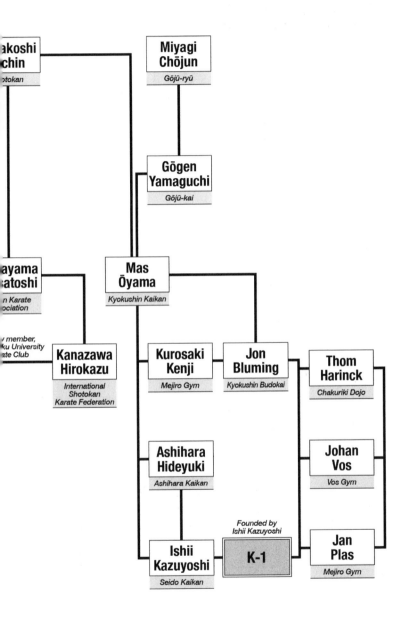

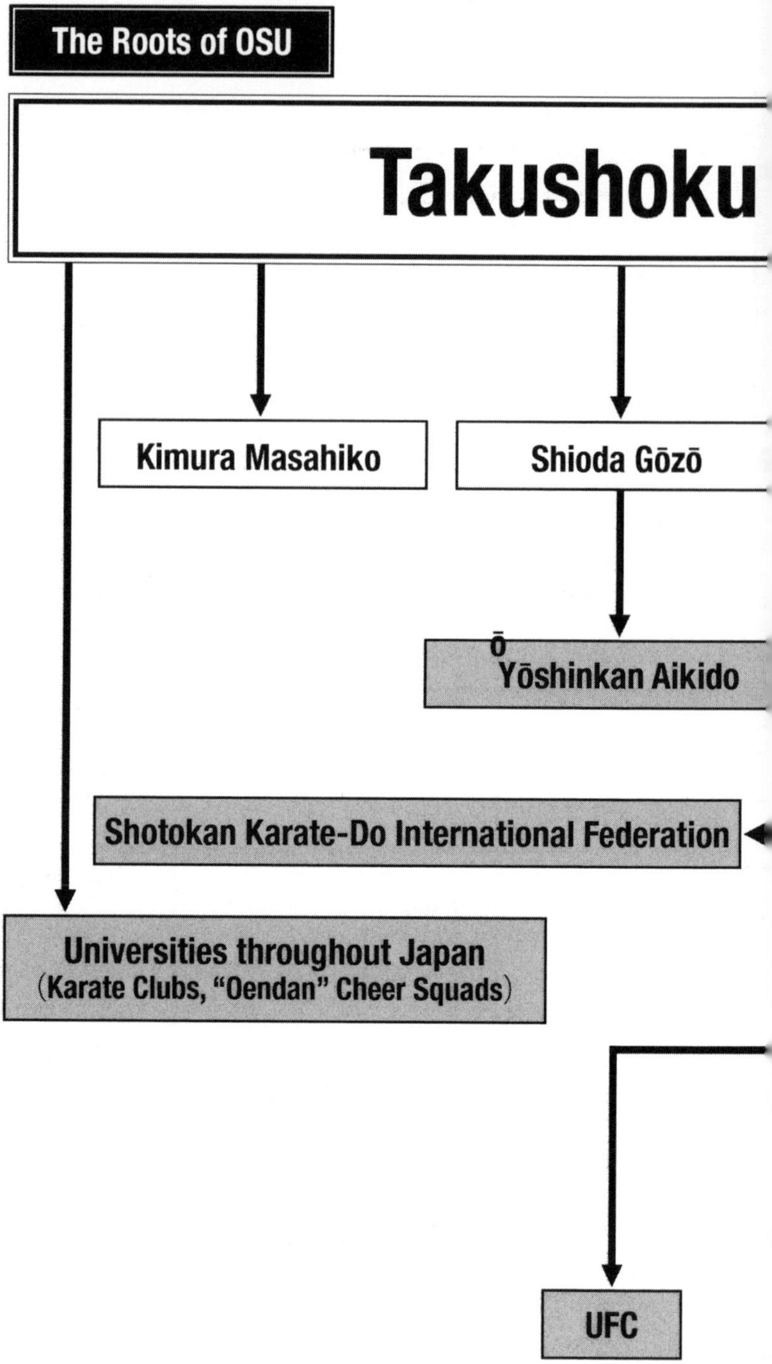

The Roots of OSU

Takushoku

Kimura Masahiko

Shioda Gōzō

Ō
Yōshinkan Aikido

Shotokan Karate-Do International Federation

Universities throughout Japan
(Karate Clubs, "Oendan" Cheer Squads)

UFC

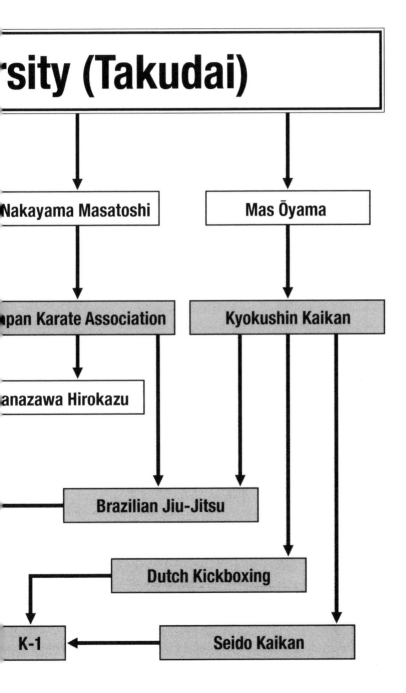

Afterword

Before and during the war, OSU embodied the realization and acceptance that life could be lost at any moment. Additionally, it symbolized the pioneering ethos of "nothing ventured, nothing gained," which was a core principle of Takudai's founding spirit.

For the first time in its history, Japan experienced the humiliation, helplessness, and despair of being under occupation after defeat in the Second World War. Takudai students serving in the military were demobilized and returned to the university. They employed the word OSU to inspire a new Takudai spirit. They put their aspirations into the two characters 押 and 忍.

Takudai alumni were at the forefront in the creation of the Japan Karate Association. Along with the subsequent spread of Shotokan karate, and Kyokushin founded by Mas Ōyama (who was also at Takudai), OSU spread beyond karate circles to other martial arts and combat sports. It was destined to become a universal phrase. Its transformation and far-reaching process of dissemination overlaps beautifully with the founding spirit of Takushoku University. This realization came as quite a revelation.

OSU later became associated with violent behavior demonstrated by college cheering squads (*ōendan*) and other groups for a period of time after the war, and young people ceased using the term because of the negative image it carried. Then, through karate, it began spreading overseas and became a universal word symbolizing peace and respect. Language indeed changes with the times.

Nevertheless, it is crucial to recognize that the origin of OSU lies in the passion and determination of the Takudai people. These brave souls departed their homeland, shouting OSU to their peers as they set sail into the unknown, uncertain if they would ever return. We should not forget the sacrifice and commitment that each of these individuals poured into the culture of OSU, and we must honor their legacy by treating their creation with reverence and respect. In other words, it is not to be taken lightly.

I humbly offer my deepest appreciation to all those who contributed to this book's publication.

OSU

References

Aoki Kiyotaka, Nakatani Yasushi, Miyamoto Tomoji, "Masatoshi Nakayama's Whole Life and His Thought of Karate-Do," *Bulletin of the Institute of Health and Sports Science*, Chuo University, 2014.

Bennett, Alexander, *Nihonjin no Shiranai Bushidō*, Bungei Shinsho, 2013.

Funakoshi Gichin, *Karatedō Ichiro*, Kōdansha, 1976.

Hikoyama Mitsuzō, *Sumō Dokuhon*, Kawade Shobō, 1952.

————*Sumōdō Sōkan*, Nihon Tosho, 1977.

Kanazawa Hirokazu, *Waga Karate Jinsei*, Nippon Budōkan, 2002.

Katō Akinori, *Densetu no Ōendan CHRONICLE*, Kawade Shobō Shinsha, 2017.

Kimura Masahiko, *Waga Jūdō*, Baseball Magazinesha, 1985.

Koike Yoshiaki, *Hagakure no Eichi: Ayamari Ichido mo Nakimono wa Ayauku Sōrō*, Kōdansha Gendai Shinsho, 1993.

——————*Hagakure - Bushi to Hōkō*, Kōdansha Gakujutsu Bunko, 1999.

Kusahara Katsuhide. *Kindai Nihon no Sekaitaiken — Nitobe Inazō no Kokorozashi to Takushoku no Seishin*, Shōgakkan Square, 2004.

——————*Nitobe Inazō 1862-1933 - Ware, Taiheiyō no Hashi to Naran*, Fujiwara Shoten, 2012.

——————*Budō Bunka to shite no Karatedō*, Fuyō Shobō Shuppan, 2019.

Kusano Fumio, *Takushoku Daigaku Hachijūnen-shi*, Takushoku Daigaku Hachijūnen-shi Kinen Jigyō Jimukyoku, 1980.

Masuda Toshinari, *Kimura Masahiko wa Naze Rikidōzan wo Korosanakatta no ka*, Shinchōsha, 2011.

Kōeki Shadan Hōjin Nihon Karate Kyōkai Rokujūgonen-shi, Nihon Karate Kyōkai Rokujūgonen-shi Hensan-Iinkai, 2014.

Nitta Ichirō, *Sumō Sono Rekishi to Gihō*, Nippon Budōkan, 2016.

Ōmori Toshinori, *OSU to wa Nanika?* Sangokan, 2016.

Royers, Fred & Scharrenberg Koen, *Legend — Oranda Kakutōka Retsuden*, Kitensha, 1997.

Takushoku Daigaku Sōritsu Hyakunen-shi Hensan Semmon Iinkai, *Takushoku Daigaku Hyakunen-shi Bukyoku Shihen*, Takushoku Daigaku, 2002.

Tamaki Benkichi, *Kaisō Yamamoto Genpō*, Shunjūsha, 1970.
Tokitsu Kenji, *Pari Kara no Budō-ron — Kokusai Bunka Toshite no Karate*, Taishūkan Shoten, 1992.

Toyoda Jō, *Kaigun Heigakkō Etajima Kyōiku*, Shinjinbutsu Ōraisha, 2010.

Watanabe Toshio, *Ajia wo Sukutta Kindai Nihonshi Kōgi — Senzen no Globalism to Takushoku Daigaku*, PHO Shinsho, 2013.

Zacharski, Andrzej Jerzy, "Kindai Okinawa Karate no Genjō to Kadai — Karateka-tachi no Mezasu Karate no Seishin-sei", University of the Ryukyus, 2019.